MANPOWER PLANNING AND CONTROL

By the same author

Salary Administration *(with D.N. Rands)*
Organization and Manpower Planning
    (now rewritten as Manpower Planning and Control)
Productivity through People

Manpower Planning and Control

Gordon McBeath

BUSINESS BOOKS
COMMUNICA - EUROPA

First published 1978

ISBN 0 220 66348 3

*This book has been set 11 on 12 point IBM Press Roman.
Printed in Great Britain by litho at The Anchor Press Ltd
and bound by Wm Brendon & Son Ltd, both of Tiptree, Essex
for the publishers, Business Books Limited
24 Highbury Crescent, London N5*

CONTENTS

PURPOSE – THE MANPOWER FUNCTION

──

1.1   Introduction

The single advantage that your organisation may have over its
competitors is in the numbers and quality of your people. If you
are in government or some non-profit making body then your cost-
effectiveness is measured partly in the number and quality of your
people.

All employers have equivalent potential access to financial and
other resources; to equipment, to technology. All decisions related
to the acquisition and use of resources will be made by your people.
The quality of the people making the decisions, and their freedom
to do so, immediately impacts on your efficiency through the
quality of the decisions they make.

Manpower represents a key decision area. Few companies know
what their manning should be, and in a large organisation, annual
manpower costs may run at a level millions of pounds above what
they should be. Just 100 too many, housed and equipped, can
cost £1 million a year.

The single advantage we have is in our people, the number and
the quality.

Numbers

The effect of carrying too many people is comparable with a man
carrying too much weight (which is perhaps why excess personnel
tend to be referred to as 'the fat'). The effect is also comparable
in that efficiency is impaired and the organisation becomes sluggish.

Consider the impact of shedding 10 per cent of your weight when you realise that you have put on much more than is comfortable. Immediately, you feel more athletic and virile — you begin winning at squash again. Most organisations can take out 10 per cent of their positions easily. A few need to take out nearer 50 per cent. Also, the company's spending power begins to be absorbed in excessive manpower costs, wages, salaries, accommodation, equipment, while capital expenditure on essential new equipment and on new product development is reduced because money is not available. At an early stage profitability is directly affected.

In contrast with the organisation slipping into obesity, we should rather be reappraising our organisation continually against up-dated objectives so that we can ensure that both organisation and manning remain purpose-designed and continually slimmed down. If we put on fat, a fast return to the slim, purpose-designed structure has to be a primary objective. Yet this is not always recognised. A typical reaction is to begin to hold wage and salary increase levels to the minimum achievable in order to try to reduce the costs of excessive manpower, but this is a further step towards disaster for the impact is immediately felt on quality.

Quality

Levels of pay set below the norms of the employment will attract and hold only the lower levels of ability in each job category. Low pay levels over any period of time have a long-term impact on the quality of employees retained. As side effects build up this trend becomes virtually impossible to reverse. Many local government and other organisations have shifted from low pay/high security packages, which were probably appropriate in the labour market for their requirements, to high pay/high security — but with no change in efficiency in view of the deeply entrenched work practices and standards which only massive restructuring can remove.

The side affects arise from the impact of lower quality people in every work situation. First, a greater number are required to do the basic work; this combines with the excessive numbers already employed and leads to increased fragmentation and production of work. Further, with lower quality people most if not all of the creative and planning type work begins to be out-dated. Non-standard events are less frequently foreseen and the managerial role drifts towards trouble-shooting rather than planning.

Most serious is the impact on job satisfaction as jobs become increasingly fragmented as work is spread between the excessive numbers of lower grade people. This results in duplication of work, continuation of obsolete activities, continued use of obsolete systems, and so on. Any remaining able people feel increasing frustration as job satisfaction levels continue to decline. Money becomes more significant as a pseudo-motivator, and pay levels begin to be pushed up for the wrong reasons without any of the advantages that normally apply in high pay situations where highly motivated and satisfied employees are found. Absenteeism is significantly high and in itself may increase manpower requirements by a further 15 per cent.

The accumulative effect can be a massive reduction in efficiency and productivity. There is an inability to compete in export markets where inefficiency offsets the advantages of a low sterling value. There are bumbling inadequacies in industrial relations that lead to large numbers of disputes and strikes; deliveries are more frequently late than not; manufacturing methods become increasingly inadequate.

Upgrading a company that has run down is not easy. The drive to do so can come only from the top and then probably through bringing in an outsider. A determined man may over 10 years make a considerable impact but change will be very difficult to achieve without changing many of the individual managers, probably more than half. Change in depth is difficult due to employee resistance and improvements can only be achieved slowly through one major change in a single function or a department at any one time.

Of course, not everyone likes the concept of working in a successful company. Apart from being profitable it will be populated by competent and, therefore, confident people (even aggressively so). Such people are inclined to tell you that they and their organisation are the best in their field, but they can hold their heads up anywhere knowing that they really are good; that their company is competitive; that it does have the edge wherever it chooses to go; and that they need never be ashamed of their performance because they will naturally have done their best. As individuals they can go anywhere for they are above average and probably they always will be, but they will not lightly join sub-standard organisations.

Manpower as a fixed investment

A decision to recruit a permanent employee is comparable with the acquisition of any other fixed asset. Your manpower loss rates may be high, but you cannot count on losing only the people you want to leave. The decision to bring in an additional man should always be taken on the assumption that he is with you to stay.

Let us consider the implications of your decision to recruit a fixed asset. One additional production operator or clerk costs around £3000 a year in wages and salaries, plus about £1000 in benefit costs, not to mention accommodation and equipment. Over

20 years, with inflation, expenditure resulting from this single
decision will be over £100,000. For a managerial slot, again over
20 years, expenditure may be approaching £500,000.

The decision to recruit and therefore commit the organisation to
this expenditure is all too frequently taken rather casually and at a
low level.

Now consider capital expenditure of £20,000 for a new machine.
There will be considerable investigation into the need for the
machine and the optimum specification, taking into account possible
future use rather than just immediate requirements. Then there will
be a written justification for the expenditure, including:

1   A financial justification, showing recovery of the investment
     within three years, or forget it.
2   How will it be financed − cash, hire purchase, hire?
3   What level of utilisation of the machine is expected?
4   How flexible is its potential use in future?
5   What are the expected operating costs?
6   Are there any potential industrial relations problems?
7   What is the obsolescence potential and what are the write-off
     plans?

Very similar questions might reasonably be asked of any single
recruitment, particularly as the commitment to expenditure is so
substantial and is becoming progressively more difficult for employers
to lay off employees who are excess to requirements or who have
obsolete skills. It is a fundamental requirement that manpower
planning should provide as many of these answers as the company
deems practical. In five years time we may well have moved on to
consider recruitment with as much care as capital expenditure.
Companies that get there first may once again be stating their
advantage over competitors.

Manpower costs in relation to income

In any organisation where the cost of manning is a significant
proportion of the income, and there can be few where this is not
so, planning and controlling that expense has to be important. It
can have a significant impact on profitability (or costs in the case
of non-commercial enterprises such as local government or
nationalised services). In labour-intensive industries and services,
staffs costs may exceed 50 per cent of income. Even in capital-
intensive industries where this figure drops towards 10 per cent
marginal overmanning must begin to cut into profits, while in
manpower-intensive units the impact of overmanning on
profitability can be disastrous. It can, for example, reduce a
potentially high profitable growth business to a loss-making static

position, where capital is absorbed by excessive manpower.

Getting manning levels right is evidently important, but we must find a balance between the arguments of economics and not ignore the people affected. There is much more to the equation as we shall see in the course of this book.

The manpower function

It is the task of manpower planning to determine and specify the optimum manning requirements now and in the forecastable future. This function fits most naturally into the personnel function, yet it is frequently separated on the grounds that personnel people are too concerned to protect people, while the task of manpower planning and control exists in a real business situation requiring commercially orientated decisions that personnel managers tend not to like. Certainly some personnel managers prefer to pick up where management has already declared a redundancy or decided on an individual severance case. They prefer to see their job as clearing up the mess rather than associating themselves with the management decision.

In the future, tough decisions on employees will be made increasingly on a combination of 'people' and 'commercial' arguments, with employees having to understand the harsh realities of international economics if they wish to continue to be secure in their jobs. But management will have to improve communications and provide a great deal of counselling, education and, of course, the facts to help this process.

1.2 The planning sequence

Business planning and organisation

Manpower planning cannot logically exist in isolation. It is a part of the whole process of management planning activity, concerned with planning the requirement and supply of the company's human resources, as distinct from financial resources, plant and equipment, and so on.

In terms of the property of the company, manpower resources include the 'intellectual property' of the company — certainly the most easily lost or misused, and needing careful planning.

Within the business planning process, a large range of assumptions will be evolved and manning requirements and supply will be related to those assumptions. Inevitably, some will be changed, but recalculation or flexing of manpower data is reasonably straight-forward.

Chapter 2 runs through the requirements of business planning and the links with manpower. It goes on to examine what is something of a middle stage — organisation. Organisation is the design we choose to structure the necessary work into functional pieces, and then on down into individual jobs. The process of reviewing the efficiency of our present organisation and how it may be affected by future business needs; of determining the changes to be made in parallel with the unfolding business plan; of adapting those plans to people and implementing the results; these are covered in the next chapter.

Manning standards and utilisation

The whole manpower planning process depends enormously on the base of manning standards. This will start with what exists and what should be, and have an in-feed of all those factors which will change current standards, including by how much and when. Without some measures of this sort no planning is possible. Most of us start with pretty crude measures and refine these as we go and as we identify the separate forecastable categories and bases for assessing rates of change.

Employee involvement is natural in determining standards of all sorts, and supervisor involvement and interest in the measures they have readily to hand on their utilisation of their own people are key factors in planning forward needs and subsequent implementation and control.

Manning standards should be developed from analysis of essential work requirements, and some form of work measurement wherever possible, and this is by no means restricted to direct manufacturing operations. Measurement can be applied in very many office or indirect situations. Where local attitudes or management style make straightforward measurement difficult, existing data in the hands of supervisors and managers can provide useful standards from an 'abbreviated' approach, which will also encourage supervisors to seek out means of improving their own utilisation of their human resources — to improve manpower productivity by better use of people.

Wherever this type of analysis is carried out, opportunities to restructure and enrich jobs should be sought in order to match people abilities to job demand, and generally heighten the level of job satisfaction. With this, comes lower manpower loss rates, lower absenteeism and generally tighter manning standards.

For all this, there is an inertia in existing standards which we must continually try to overcome. Our concern for improving the use of people, with close participation of supervisors and managers may be the secret of radical improvement in our overall manning quality as well as numbers. This is an area for experimentation and development of what works in your environment.

Manpower requirement planning

Manpower planning follows on from the establishment of the main assumptions in the business plan. Once we know the rough level of sales volumes and mix, the manufacturing schedules required, the research and development programmes, we are well on the way to applying our manning standards to establish the manpower require-ments that go with the assumed levels of activity. We should have built-in assumptions about the organisation structures to be used and the effect of these on the levels of manpower required should be determined.

The plans will be set out with total numbers, but behind the summary will be detailed schedules by precise categories and skills and levels for every function. This detail will be necessary as a starting point when the questions of supply planning are tackled.

Whever possible, manpower requirement planning must be based on manning standards associated with work demand factors to facilitate flexing. The abbreviated approach is just as useful as a guide. In the absence of measured standards, the extention of existing actual 'standards' (good or bad) by using crude ratios of people to work on a trend line can give a useful guide to the area of numbers required.

Development of contingency plans for fringe options or probabilities and plans to enable unplanned sudden increases or decreases in work volume form part of requirement planning.

Manpower information system

Modern management depends on comprehensive data on subjects on which it may be called to make decisions. Too frequently, manpower is the poor relation in the management information stakes, but recognition of need is changing this.

For any system, specification of required inputs and outputs is essential. In building up the data base, coding of employment data for ready access and analysis is critical, and the CODOT system can provide the basic answer, with scope for embellishment if required.

Data on absenteeism and overtime is an essential part of the system, if a little apart from the more static data base. These are factors that have a direct impact on manpower requirements.

Whom do we employ; what skills do they have; how good are they; how are they developing? These are just some of the questions to which we need answers. Much of the analysis should fall out from the basic information system, but the impact of loss rates and promotion patterns is altering the current inventory all the time.

Taking the 'inventory' and assessing the rate and form of change are vital to the questions of manpower supply, for what we cannot provide from within, we must seek out from other sources.

The use of appraisal of performance, assessment of future potential, and the use of psychological tests, are all part of the armoury we use to get the answers we need.

Manpower supply planning

This is the 'crunch' point, where we bring together all the data we have on our future requirements and on our present manpower 'stock' and the ways we expect it to change. From these analyses, we see the future supply problems be detailed by function, category, skill and level. These show our future recruitment needs, highlight our need to increase the promotion rates of some categories by intensive training and development; show retraining and redeployment needs and highlight the excess of staff who are likely to become redundant.

In all these areas we need positive action programmes to back up recognised needs. We must be sure that the actions required are taken and are successful, otherwise basic assumptions within the business plan may be adversely affected.

Manpower control and audit

The philosophy throughout this book is one of planning ahead as a basis for control and audit. The logic of controls on every aspect of manning should be evident. We are dealing with an expensive resource that can be easily misused or underutilised. Controls quietly ensure that we continually try to use these resources in the best ways possible.

Controls are exercised on current actions and decisions. We subsequently audit the results to be sure that the intended result has been achieved and that controls are not being by-passed or critical decisions ignored. This happens far more than we expect where there is little or no audit, so the importance of the audit function is evident.

'Above a certain level, manpower planning ceases to be a matter
of numbers by category, and becomes linked to individual positions
and individual incumbents.'

For the top slice of the company, we are dealing with a combination
of business development, organisation development and individual
career development. It must be handled with considerable care, by
unbiased and imaginative executives, and take into account the
employees' viewpoints and preferences if it is to be a workable plan.

Manpower planning and concern for people

In an imaginary situation where only commercial criteria apply
people could be treated as just another asset and equated with
machines, which can be purchased or hired, scrapped or reconditioned,
cannibalised, transferred to new locations and so on, at the sole
discretion of management, thus ensuring appropriate facilities for
all situations are provided at all times. In reality we know that we
cannot treat our human assets in this way, at least not without their
full support and participation. Given that support (or at least
knowledgable acceptance), decisions to recruit or make redundant,
to develop, to retrain, to transfer are all possible, but we need to
understand the limitations that people and legislation impose on the
free use of these assets.

As employers or as managers, we accept important social
responsibilities for our employees, not only immediately but for
their future. To an increasing extent we take responsibility for
ensuring their future employment. By planning our future
manning requirements and careful subsequent analyses of the
manpower we have, we can take people into our confidence at
an early stage regarding changes in our markets, and order
position, or the changing technology of how we make our products;
in fact all significant factors that influence the employment of our
people. Then, with involvement, we can determine the required
action, such as needs and opportunities for retraining and redeployment for as many of those adversely affected by change as may
wish to take that course and for whom there will be jobs.
Management has a responsibility to persuade and encourage
acceptance of change in an environment of change, and in the
process it cannot afford to forget that all employees consider
that they have the right to work.

Seen from the employee's viewpoint the extent to which
organised labour has developed over the past few years is an
additional insurance that management will accept its social

10 responsibilities fully. Much organised labour reaction can be seen
as defence against possible management lack of fairness or lack
of sufficient respect for the rights of employees. To an increasing
extent legislation is backing up the organised labour position and
ensuring management's acceptance of social responsibility, for
example through the Employment Protection Act. The concluding
comment on this subject is that we have to plan and handle
correctly our industrial relations strategy to ensure that we identify
all the things we need to do, how we will do them, and their
acceptability to our employees.

BUSINESS PLANNING AND ORGANISATION

2.1 Business planning

Business planning is the foundation of all continuing successful
business operations. The company that knows where it is going, is
prepared for all eventualities and controls its course against this
background is most likely to produce consistently good results in
all its activities.

Planning evolves from an acceptance of the inevitability
of change. For example, people change, or rather develop, and as
they develop they cease to be content with their previous level of
work and seek broader responsibilities. Apart from changes in
people, few companies are content to rest on their laurels, satisfied
with their products and with their share of the market. New ideas,
new products and new marketing methods constantly alter the
balance against the interests of the stagnating company and against
any hope of standing still.

Planning provides an early warning system against all the things
that may happen to us. It enables us to make assessments of the
resistance that may occur against changes that may be inevitable
and enables us to prepare the way to ensure that the essential changes
are made timely and effectively.

To be effective planning must be soundly based, systematic and
comprehensive. The business plan must be feasible, not decorative.
If it is to be realistic it must be based on a full study of the current
business situation and factors likely to influence the business in
the future. Such a study is highly complex with many variables and
alternatives. A worthwhile result is only likely to emerge from a
systematic approach involving the selection, collection and analysis

of all relevant data. One begins by setting out the raw materials of
the study:
1   The substantial volume of basic information on the current
     business and all known changes.
2   The assumptions on all future trends, technological develop-
     ments and competitive actions.
3   The company's broad objectives, such as the achievement of
     a defined share of a particular market.
In particular the assumptions must be digested systematically and
an assessment made regarding the relevance and importance of each
one to the division or company. The possible future lines of business
development gradually emerge. The various options get evaluated in
greater or lesser detail, for example a product may be developed to
a sales volume of £50,000 or £5,000,000 depending on the
availability of different but assessable levels of resources.

It is unlikely that available resources will be adequate to meet the
whole range of business possibilities across the company. An analysis
of these possibilities, requirements for capital and other resources,
and so on, then follows. From the results of these analyses decisions
must be taken regarding the best buy in order to make optimum
use of resources available for both the short-term and the long-term
good of the company. It is at this all-embracing stage when the
factors, variables and alternatives are so many that some medium
and large organisations may use computer analyses of variables and
options to guide their decisions.

Business planning procedure needs to involve a whole management
team with an input from every function.

Business control is the natural corollary to business planning. A
business needs information in order to plan. Having prepared precise
plans, it is logical, if management is to be purposeful, to maintain a
control over what actually happens, using the same information
sources to observe variations from plans, and having observed
variation, to analyse and take action.

We now look briefly at business planning procedures, and then
more closely at the factors that influence change, before going on
into organising planning.

Business planning procedure

A description of the complete process of business planning would
be out of place here. It is, however, necessary to understand the
process, which is a continuous one. There is no end point or final
conclusion, but only an endless reappraisal.

The process is systematic in that it follows a logical procedure
which brings all relevant data under scrutiny at regular intervals;

but it also includes arrangements for special studies of particular
requirements and interests. Throughout the year, specialists may
be studying product costing, or marketing analyses, and so on,
which are potentially relevant to the company's overall planning
ideas, but go much deeper than is normally required for the plan.

The business plan 'events' provide periodic culminations of
activity, which bring together as complete a picture of what exists
and what may exist as the company can envisage and obtain. If
data sources concerning the existing activities, assumptions and
outside influences fall short of requirements, then the basis for
planning is restricted. If, for example, the marketing analysis is too
coarse, or the knowledge of production capacity does not state the
degree of facility to change from product A to product B, or the
information on competitor activity is inadequate, then there may
be insufficient data on which key decisions and assumptions can
be made.

Planning draws out the views of all the specialists and managers
capable of making original contributions to the problems being
examined. From the studies involved, senior management must
appraise the advice of specialists and subordinates, taking their
broader view over the enterprise, and state which course of action
shall be planned for on each significant issue. In doing so, they will
do more than simply absorb the statistics and assumptions presented
to them, and may trigger off a series of 'choice' studies, covering
the effects of alternative courses of action. For example, while the
company's resourses will permit a certain amount of growth, how
should these resources be deployed in order to achieve the best
longer-term results? The various possible lines of growth will soak
up differing volumes of the separate resources, some being heavier
on finance, or personnel, than others. The final decision must aim
at producing the best short- and long-term benefits for the company.

Factors that influence planning

Business planning is founded on what exists, and develops to fit
what is expected to exist. It establishes a set of assumptions and
intentions based on all those factors that may influence the way in
which the company's basic objectives may be attained, or even
influence the form of the basic objectives themselves. These factors
fall under a number of functional headings which we examine below.
It is unlikely that any of these will be found in isolation as, for
example, a breakthrough in product design will bring problems of
financial requirements, of production, and of manpower.

Technological development   Most industries today are faced with rapid changes of technologies, some of which are evolving at an almost phenomenal pace. Some developments in the electronics industry, for instance, are superseded so fast that many products may be technically obsolete before they reach the production stage.

In this type of situation, companies must be dynamic and flexible to survive, and organisation can only be planned ahead in broad terms with readiness to respond to immediate and urgent, unforeseen requirements. The unexpected can mean anything from a change in a manufacturing process to a completely new product resulting from a development which makes the previous one obsolete. New methods and processes place heavy demands on production engineering skills; automatic processing replaces production operatives; production management requirements change. These things can be seen to be happening and the effects on organisational structures acted upon.

Technological and product changes also affect markets and marketing methods. Market planning responsibility includes identification of potential new products based on existing technology as well as research to find new markets for existing products. If a new product or new market requires a different selling approach, an organisation capable of providing the right approach must be developed.

A major factor in forward planning is *development in manufacturing practice,* especially in automated processes. However, the very substantial cost of new equipment may restrict the pace of advance. Athough automation is a natural development of mass production the manpower and industrial relations impact of automation plans always require careful analysis.

We are interested in several aspects of manufacturing development. New methods of production may be required for old products, yet may not require organisational change. Many new processes do alter manpower requirements, in both types and numbers, and may change organisational and control demands. The effects of manufacturing development decisions must be clearly appreciated in advance, particularly as their influence on manpower requirements in the production shops may have a substantial effect on the shape of organisation and control required.

Changes in volume required create particular problems in manufacturing (as is frequently visible in the motor industry). Existing facilities may be appropriate for the new volumes, but changes in manning and in shift and overtime working may be necessary. Usually contingency plans should exist to cover the actions required, and the manpower and cost implications.

Changing equipment/employee ratios alters the basis on which an organisation has been designed. *Employee–supervisory* ratios change and machine utilisation levels become more important. If

there has been substantial investment in capital equipment, employee
time ceases to be the most expensive item in the cost breakdown
and management interest and activity are more concerned with
optimising the use of expensive equipment, and new requirements
for shift working may be imposed.

Market development　I have covered some of the effects of changing
technologies on marketing. There are also gradual changes in
traditional markets. The basic tool to meet this situation is an
effective economic and marketing research service which makes a
careful assessment of each situation.

From this forward look, marketing direction can be restyled to
meet the anticipated events. Marketing organisations must always
be flexible and adaptive − provided, of course, that the decision
making and changes are always coldly logical and not over reactive.

Marketing strategy will be closely related to the actions of
competitors in the same field. Where two or more companies share
a market and any one decides to increase its share of the market, the
marketing situation may be considered to have changed significantly.

Competitors must be assumed to be examining the same problems;
considering the same moves; to be coming to the same general
conclusions on the overall situation. As you keep an eye on them, so
they will be watching you, assessing your strategies, building up a
profile of your probable development and future products. If your
actions become too stylised, too easily forecastable, competitors
may anticipate your plans and outmanoeuvre you. Marketing planning
must be dynamic and imaginative, yet based on down-to-earth
analyses of the actual marketing situations and problems.

The marketing situation will have been analysed, using the
normal techniques (although it is accepted that these may be
misleading in respect of new product lines and new markets).
We need, for example, to know the potential market, for once
saturation point can be foreseen, a change to replacement selling
must be planned. Similarly, changing profit margins and pressures
on pricing will influence selling methods, as lower margins may be
offset by higher sales volume, although other factors may then
influence the situation. The effect of changing selling techniques
on field sales forces and marketing support staff organisation
emerges from specific studies.

Perhaps most important in marketing planning are the
preparations made for launching of new products. For certain types
of products a manager may be appointed three years or more in
advance of release so that he may plan and build the new product
marketing arrangements.

Economic factors　In recent years, various metal prices have fluctuated substantially, with higher prices tending to reduce demand as other materials become economically viable for some applications.

As one material ceases to be economically sound for a particular application at a particular price, a demand for technological change is thus imposed. Such an event should be foreseen, and trends in raw material prices should be watched to provide foreknowledge of a likely increase in price above the critical level, while outline plans for alternative product lines are investigated.

Both national and international trends on relevant economic factors must be watched. Especially important may be trends in wage and salary levels, or social security costs, which may influence the usage of people, price levels, and so on. At some stage, it may prove more economic to utilise an automatically controlled production line rather than use substantially greater numbers of machine operators. Or it may be logical to establish manufacture in a low-cost country for manpower-intensive activities.

In considering new locations, unaccustomed levels of wages and salaries may make an enterprise less profitable than expected, while difficulties may also arise owing to the length and cost of transport lines and communication.

General taxation changes, or changes in legislation – such as alterations in import and export controls and charges – may sometimes be anticipated as possibilities, depending on whether they take the form of emergency measures, or represent an evolutionary move.

Where special legislation applies locally, for the purpose of boosting new industry in an area, promoting an export drive or some other defined objective, it is usually less likely to change, so giving a known period of stability. Overseas, however, some of the less developed countries have followed periods of trade encouragement with excessive control, or nationalisation.

Financial resources   An established organisation with sound and marketable products is likely to be able to obtain any reasonable amount of financial support. It will, however, wish to make quite sure that the resultant return on investment, from each aspect of a project, is acceptable in relation to both the short- and long-term interests of the company.

A new product may require up to £10 million to develop, produce and launch, with an operational loss expected from the new line for three years or more. If the company backing the project is sure of the long-term future, it may be willing to invest the necessary money, but it is not going into an unprofitable venture simply because it has the resources for growth.

If an activity is unprofitable and likely to remain so, there is little

economic sense in continuing its operation. Exceptionally, prestige
reasons may be considered to justify the continuation of a loss-
making subsidiary, but this is rare. Taking a less extreme example,
a company which is insufficiently profitable needs to take a close
look at itself and trim off some of the fat, particularly manpower
involved on non-essential work.

This aspect of manpower is important. Basically, almost any
operation can be done in a simple way, with a minimum of staff.
But many activities may be carried out more elegantly, using
sophisticated procedures to produce more elaborate results, which
require more people, and therefore costs more. While company
operation remains reasonably profitable, the supplementary detail
may be considered worthwhile, but an unprofitable year − or,
particularly, more than one − will see a drastic change in this
attitude and a close look at the past growth of non-essential services.

The finance function is as much affected by operational change
as any other function. The company with half-a-dozen large
customers, which adjusts its trading to deal directly with a large
number of new small customers, needs a strong credit control
function for the first time, plus a greater degree of machine
accounting, not to mention changes in invoicing procedures and
additional staff. These requirements have to be anticipated.

Personnel resources   The feasibility of any particular business
plan is dependent on the availability of personnel. To take an
extreme example, the creation of a new factory in the Highlands
of Scotland would founder on lack of personnel unless housing
and other substantial amenities could be provided to attract the
necessary personnel. Thus, in general terms, the plan must assume
that the company can attract the appropriate types of personnel
to the location concerned at the right time and price (and include
a detailed manpower supply plan). It is potentially dangerous to
leave plans hedged with some doubts, even if there are good
prospects of resolving difficulties. The planned answer has to be
there so that, if it proves wrong, this fact is identified immediately.

The real problems arise from non-availability of experienced and
competent managers, and this applies both to new enterprises and
to existing structures. The question 'Have we got, or can we obtain,
managers capable of running the organisation required and achieving
their objectives in the fullest sense?', has to have a satisfactory
answer.

*Personnel resources place a very real limit on the growth potential
of a company.* Where existing personnel are working at the limits of
their capacities, growth cannot be planned and carried through on a
sound basis unless additional suitable managerial or other essential
talent can be obtained. Where relevant competence cannot be

obtained outside, it may sometimes be made available from a temporary regrouping of existing responsibilities internally, designed to increase specialisation and concentrate the available special experience on the urgent situations.

The almost frightening dependence on one key man which results is a sure way of encouraging maximum development of good supporting staffs. A business plan showing rapid growth with its accompanying need for additional staff of specific types, requires a clear subsidiary plan which will guarantee the availability of an adequate manpower supply, from whatever source.

2.2 Organisation planning

Business planning is concerned with the forward planning of the entire commercial enterprise covering every aspect of its future. Within this planning process the design of the organisational shape best suited to the achievement of the business objectives is an important first step. In most situations organisation change is gradual, evolving as the company and its people mature and as the outlook on organisation matters changes. In many large groups there is a cyclical swing between centralisation and decentralisation, for example, which serves to wash away the worst of each at the opposite extremes of the swing. However, it is necessary to plan the evolution and ensure that the structure remains purpose-built to achieve objectives and is slimmed-down for optimum efficiency.

An organisation plan is an acknowledgement of anticipated change in the business and is the planned sequence of adjustments to organisation to meet the new objectives.

Organisation planning is essentially a long-term activity concerned with a developing situation over, perhaps, five years ahead and the means of how to move from the present structure towards the future ideal. In setting the pace of this evolution the availability and readiness of suitable personnel are of critical importance – so much so that people may be considered the only determining factor in the timing of the plan. This emphasises the close relationship between organisation planning and the various aspects of manpower planning. While emphasising the long-term nature of organisation planning this activity will draw attention to immediate organisation problems and short-term implications which directly affect people and therefore have emotional implications, which are very different from actions designed to improve the distant future.

The analytical process of reviewing organisation requirements, planning a new or revised shape and implementing decision, is basically identical whether the application is immediate or gradual. The difference arises where urgency forces immediate action of an uncomfortable nature, where planned change over a longer period might have been kinder to individuals and easier to digest. Resistance to such change may force slower action or acceptance of some compromise plan which defers a proportion of the change for more gradual acceptance. Implementation of organisation change is examined separately at the end of this section.

The organisation planning process falls into three stages:

1 Analysis of the purpose and form of the present organisation, of its failings and of the new and potential influences upon it.
2 Planning logical organisation shapes theoretically capable of achieving the company's future objectives, but flexible enough to adapt to possible developments and susequently planning how they may be manned.
3 Implementing the agreed changes.

These headings equally fit the pattern of an organisation review over the whole period of a five-year business plan, or a one-off corrective-action type review. Critical re-appraisal of a continual nature follows the same stages. Sometimes activity under all three headings may be proceeding at one time at various paces covering various parts of a company's operations.

Organisation analysis

Studies of existing organisation and current organisational require-ments are going on all the time. For example, it is probably rare for any management level vacancy to be filled without some analysis of the requirements of the job, now and in the short-term future, to ensure that the job and man specification used for purposes of replacement are as up-to-date as possible.

Organisations are constantly changing – so much so that one can reasonably be sure of finding something seriously wrong with a structure that has remained theoretically unchanged for five years and pretty likely to find problems after even two years of static structure.

Gradual modifications in requirements for technical development as well as turnover of people combine to ensure change and here I am thinking as much of the minor changes in relationships which may be outside the limits of major forward planning.

We must know what the organisation or unit is designed to achieve and where it fits in with other units if we are to be constructive in our review. If there is any doubt about objectives or purpose, or if these have recently been changed, there is a reasonable prospect that any problem that exists stems from this.

The first requirement then is to review the existing objectives and re-establish them, either in the old or in a revised form. We must ensure that they are meaningful, that they are precise, that they are not in conflict with other parts of the company and that the organisational unit with which we are concerned has a clear purpose. Next we should examine the objectives of the various functions or departments to ensure that these are designed to achieve their subsidiary objectives and that they represent a logical division of activities. We should ensure that there appears to be comprehensive coverage of all the things that need to be done and that duplication is avoided.

It may be that at this stage of a study a flaw is identified in the existing organisation. Indeed, it may have been this flaw that triggered off the study. This may require immediate correction before the main study is continued to determine long-term objectives.

More often organisational thoughts are brought to mind only during the studies. Splintered fragments of a function separated from the main activity may be easily apparent, but when the thoughts lie in the sub-grouping or around personalities the study becomes more complex. Answers to these problems come primarily from job analysis.

The collection of job information for this purpose is relatively straightforward. The analyst obtains his picture of objectives from the department manager, from the manager of the next highest level and perhaps also from supporting staff, checking out any obvious conflicts or differences as he goes along. Further, he obtains at the same time a current set of job analysis forms that gives him a complete picture of current activities and responsibilities. He then sits down quietly to match one against the other.

This task is not done quickly, especially where the span of the review is wide and the level in the organisation being examined is high. Individual interpretation of actual roles varies at least marginally and one is working all the time with slightly blurred lines.

Out of the study comes a patchwork with current assignments set out over the logical requirements. Segments of work that have broken away from their main group are highlighted on an analysis chart, perhaps by the use of separate colours for different functions. The blank areas which no-one properly covers will also stand out, as will the heavily marked areas of duplicated activity and confused responsibility, perhaps between staff and line. This chart provides a basis for re-drawing areas of responsibility to clarify which post is responsible for each activity. At the end we should know that all activities required are properly covered, that none are overlooked nor duplicated, that the work grouping in use is at least effective and that relationships between staff and line and with other departments are clearly understood and acceptable.

Before we leave job analysis, a valuable part of an organisation review is the study of the job grading schedule or preferably a

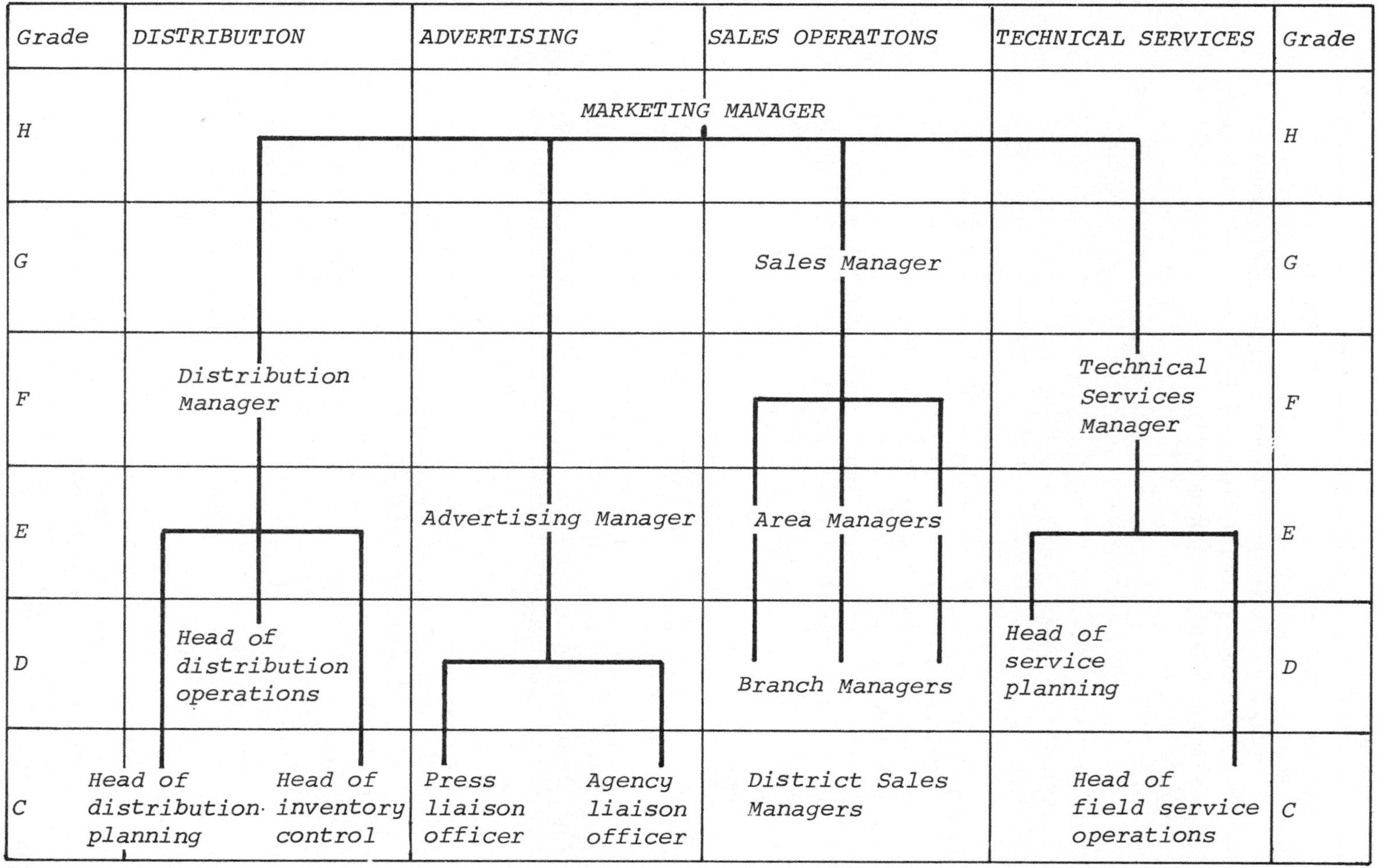

Grade	DISTRIBUTION	ADVERTISING	SALES OPERATIONS	TECHNICAL SERVICES	Grade
H			MARKETING MANAGER		H
G	Distribution Manager		Sales Manager		G
F		Advertising Manager		Technical Services Manager	F
E	Head of distribution operations	Press liaison officer	Area Managers	Head of service planning	E
D	Head of inventory control	Agency liaison officer	Branch Managers		D
C	Head of distribution planning		District Sales Managers	Head of field service operations	C

Figure 2.1 Stratified organisation chart

stratified organisation chart in which all jobs in the organisation are shown in a value relationship one to another as well as reporting relationship (see Figure 2.1).

Where the relationship between supervisory and subordinate grades and salaries deviates from an acceptable pattern difficulties may arise. A salary relationship between supervisor and subordinate of three to two is considered acceptable and where intervals between salary values of job grades are of the order of 20 per cent one would expect to find supervisor/subordinate differentials in steps of two grades. If the study shows an area with consistent one-grade intervals between jobs this will tend to be taken as a strong danger signal justifying further investigation. There is little doubt that the individuals personally involved in the structure would be very much aware of the problem and of the need for rationalising the reporting structure.

On the other hand, a department with three, four or even five grades between the manager and his subordinates is equally in difficulty. The difference in work level involves the manager in a volume of work at too low a level while some of his subordinates will be stretched to do some work at a level far above their average level. This situation may result from a growth structure where the effect of the rising level of the top job was understood organisation-ally and the need for an intermediate level was overlooked. An intermediate level plus a re-allocation of responsibilities should provide a solution.

The problems of growth organisation are easily flagged by grading. Where a division is growing very fast the size of the top jobs will also grow. While one hopes that the individuals in those jobs will grow too, this does not always happen. Then the job, as carried out by a limited individual, may remain static and inhibit the growth potential of the division. The inevitable result of this is recognition of the need for a more highly graded post to carry out the newly grown border responsibilities.

On the fringe of any organisation study are the local anomalies. The most obvious are the personal assistants, assistant managers or deputies, or one-over-one reporting relationships. Each of these may be a special arrangement designed to meet specific organi-sational situations and problems, but they should never be permitted to continue after the original purpose has been dealt with. Nor should they ever be accepted without strong justification. Any excess will disturb the smooth running of an organisation and will require remedial attention.

The end result of an organisation study is likely to be definition of a structure plus a set of job descriptions, plus associated employee specifications. These are obviously the ideal requirements and organisation structures attempt to ignore the personalities of the people who actually fill the boxes. Unfortunately, or perhaps fortunately for most of us, this ideal is rarely attained and we have to accept that any organisation structure will adapt to some extent to the requirements of the people in and around it. We all know examples of organisations built around or adapted to fit a particular individual. When this does occur the individual is perhaps a senior specialist with an exceptionally strong personality who has a unique value to the company. The organisation reacts to make maximum use of this special individual.

The organisation built round such an individual is obviously special. It is permitted because it will be effective due to the particular talents of the central figure. No general guidance on the type of organisation structure to use can be given. More to the point is what happens when the spell is broken and the key man is no longer there. As he will be irreplacable the organisation built round the man ceases to be relevant. Even the objectives of the unit may change at the same time.

One must also watch for the odd organisation that is too odd. A senior executive may wish to link his marketing development and manufacture on product group lines and produce an acceptable structure. On the other hand, if he proposes to merge the personnel function with finance, expecting personnel to be no more than an administrative activity, his judgement may prove faulty.

Apart from the effect on structure of one outstanding individual a shortage of a particular type of skill may result in similar pressures. Within a computer applications department, for example, it may be necessary to structure the work to increase the training role of all experienced personnel in order to pass on experience to as wide a range of people as quickly as possible.

The pressures for change

The starting point for any review of new pressures on organisation must be a list of all the assumptions recorded in the business plan. If the plan is comprehensive, the assumptions are likely to have been recorded by function and one can work through these, testing the possible impact on forward organisation requirements.

In marketing, the assumptions about the strength of competitor activity covering all our product areas and all the geographic areas in which we plan to sell are highly relevant to the type, scale and quality of our own marketing organisation. From the finance part of the plan the section on changed pricing strategy may similarly impact on our own marketing organisation requirements.

In manufacture, unchanged total manpower numbers may have been expanded to show massive change in skills mix required. This will impact on the supervisory organisation within manufacture, but much more significantly on the need to strengthen a personnel department to cover increased industrial relations pressures and increased retraining and redeployment. By this approach we can be sure of identifying all relevant factors.

Organisation planning rides in the wake of business planning as a restyling exercise to ensure that the company is prepared for the changing requirements and can attain any new planned objectives set. To summarise the analysis stage of the exercise we are concerned with assessing, precisely, (1) the organisation we have and (2) the pressures for change.

Before developing the forward plan, the current and urgent problems of ineffective structures must be tackled. The organisation man gains no kudos from proposing long-term answers while short-term inadequacies are left untackled.

Urgent situations usually stem from individuals in the form of personality problems or performance failure, or from some radical business development that will not tolerate much delay in action. A company with an established planning system can usually digest a problem as existing plans are likely to have given some thought to almost any contingency.

The most fascinating task facing the organisation planner is that of taking a long view ahead. To some people, sketching the future organisation may seem a speculative game with individuals as pawns. Future organisation and managers are critically important and their planning is both essential to the company and highly confidential, but can we really forecast ahead.

The answer to this is not a simple 'yes'. We cannot be certain that our estimates of the impact of all the variables influencing organisation will be correct. An error in one or more of them may have a substantial effect on future requirements and organisation shape, but if the degree of error on each facet is kept to a minimum the overall picture should be basically sound and as the plan unfolds and is continually reassessed against the assumptions made there is continual scope for amending the organisation plan itself. Everything depends on the depth of thinking which goes into the groundwork.

The development in organisation for the 12 months immediately ahead is vitally important and planning should be very accurate. Most of the major developments likely to impact on our organisation requirements three to five years ahead should already be apparent so that our organisation plan can be expected to be reasonably accurate. In the long term, say ten years ahead, the fundamental changes to come may well have begun to emerge, but many other developments will be less visible. Further, the timing of various breakthroughs will be uncertain so that while the long-term organisation plans can be developed, it is likely that the timing of their implementation will be the major uncertainty.

Planning ahead 12 months is very similar to a review of current organisation. The procedure differs only in that we must foresee the impact of pressures and adapt to be ready for them rather than react when they have begun to hurt. Planning ahead to a substantially changed situation expected three to five years hence involves all the skills of organisation planning. Over such a period all current faults can be planned out of existence and all future requirements may be met by the use of normal organisational components designed for their specific purpose. If necessary the fine detail of the future organisation can be filled in in terms of job descriptions, forecast objectives and future employee specifications, so that the further stage of long-term management manpower planning may be followed through.

The theoretical requirement

This three-to-five year forecast provides us with an opportunity to virtually ignore all existing structures and people and concentrate on the ideal organisation for various points in the future. This is a deliberately theoretical exercise which will subsequently enable us to recognise imperfections in our structure that may resist growth potential or effectiveness.

The theoretical plan of future organisations starts with the business plan, the broad view of company objectives and the detailed summary of specific year-by-year objectives for each function and department. The theoretical organisation plan sets out ideal structures with logical groupings of functions and divisions of responsibilities and optimum shape for the co-ordination of effort and achievement of objectives. Achievement of the company's business objectives requires division of objectives into parts that can be achieved by appropriately skilled groups or individual employees. It is possible for the work required to achieve these objectives to be allocated to functions and sub-functions through a series of stages. This process can be followed through in great detail as each basic piece of each function is taken and broken down into smaller, more specialised activities. The work requirement against each can be sketched out and the subsidiary structure developed. Indeed it is possible to carry the exercise through to the point where we arrive at a total theoretical structure within which each single post, down to a chosen level, is determined and defined. In an organisation planning exercise this detail may be of little value, but its application to manpower planning is important. Its value is greatest in enabling us to build up a complete picture of the end-result of a major organisation change so that the precise end-product is defined. Further detailed planning is necessary, of course, to determine how to get from the present structure to the required future structure.

Theory into practice

Organisation is essentially about people, as is demonstrated in some detail in Section 9.4 at the end of this book. The stylised structure may at first look beautifully neat and tidy, but rather different after the people factor has been added to it. The skills and abilities of existing staff rarely match the requirements of the theoretical structure.

Even where there is a period of several years in which to prepare the staffing of the ideal structure, the problems of assembling a group of exactly right people at exactly the right time could achieve only momentary success quickly unbalanced by the individual development and changing organisation requirements.

Individuals, however, also provide an inertia against organisation change which must be gradually circumvented in order to achieve each step in the evolutionary plan. The implementation phase of organisation planning is concerned with the detailed phasing-in of the adjustments necessary to approach the ideal. The objective might be achieved by one catastrophic change, but the effect on morale, productivity, security and stability, may throw out the whole balance of the structure which would then require further reappraisal within a short time.

A logical organisation structure, however carefully designed to meet the special requirements of the situation, is still a long way from being an effective operational structure. In the early stages of the exercise the creation has been largely theoretical, perhaps in large companies developed by organisation analysts and involving general managers and a range of senior executives. A proportion of these people have functional loyalties, say to finance or production, and may place these loyalties ahead of the overall interests of the company.

At the long-range planning stage these difficulties are only in the background. There is plenty of time to overcome disputed points but when change is imminent we must face up to the reasons why proposals cannot work — to the personalities, to the politics, to resistance to change, in fact to all the hell fire one meets whenever one attempts to change organisation.

It may take time to persuade all the interested people that it is their study conforming to their requirements and in their interest, but this seems the only way. Once they take credit for the design no one is going to stop them making the change they have planned.

In this process some minor adjustments may be necessary which may well produce an improved final result.

An analysis of the points to be solved and an identification of the individuals likely to be adversely affected helps the selling. I have found that a number of individual discussions with the more senior people concerned enables much of the proposal to be negotiated confidentially, piece by piece, over a short period of time. A hard core of problems can be gradually isolated. Probably these were anticipated anyway and manoeuvres planned from an early stage to deal with them. They are likely to centre around individuals (which leads us into career planning) and the entire sales strategy should be planned around the handling of these people. If career side-tracking or demotion is involved, it may be proposed to dress up the move as a promotion, but it is preferable for the employee's manager to face him honestly, fully briefed and with the complete story of the move planned and of everything it will involve. There is never long-term advantage in failing to face up to a personal situation of this sort. Failing to do so leads only to loss of respect and authority.

The handling of this stage is subject to few other rules. Analyse the situation and plan your approach on the knowledge of the people with whom you will have to deal and your own personal ways of handling people and situations. When the organisation study is completed and implemented, the concluding touch will be a publication to all those who need to know about the change.

MANNING STANDARDS AND UTILISATION

Any forecast of manning requirements must involve assumptions about the work that will be required and the amounts of work that can be done by an employee or group of the relevant category. The relationships between these two represent the manning standards to be used for planning purposes.

Identification of the work to be done and subsequent measurement of standards is relatively easier in direct producing or in routine activities, and relatively more difficult in jobs with greater discretionary elements and less easily definable activities.

In direct production, given a required volume of output that can be divided into known work units previously work studied, the number of standard hours required to complete the work is easily calculated. Assumptions can be made for minor changes in production methods and time standards closely related to current experience. The end result is likely to be a forecast with a high degree of accuracy.

In administrative activities with a high proportion of variable elements in the work, it is still possible to measure the time required with some degree of accuracy. However, the analysis required will take much longer in order to pick up the full range of activities embodied in the job. For example, a job with a cycle time of a month would need to be studied, part-time, over the full cycle. Many accounting posts have such a cycle time between production of monthly accounts; to cover every aspect the study would need to take into consideration the production of the annual accounts.

Many departments are fully occupied or overloaded because a proportion of their time is spent on unnecessary work. In reviewing manning requirements, it is always worth asking once again 'Is all the work really necessary?' Almost always, the short answer is that there are various activities which have ceased to be required, or are duplicated, or could be simplified. If some additional work is required, you may be sure it will be asked for, but somehow, nobody looks round for what can be trimmed out — until a manpower analyst comes round.

Time spent on trimming back work requirements to the necessary minimum will improve the manning standards at the end. There can be no satisfaction for an employee in knowing that the work he or she is doing has no impact on anything or anybody and can be deposited immediately in the rubbish bin. It does not follow that there is immediate redundancy for the unfortunate employee. In all normal circumstances, natural wastage is likely to provide redeployment opportunities within a short time, with the knowledge that the new work is essential to the ongoing operation of the enterprise.

Study of the work to be done might also take into account more detailed organisation and methods analysis to ensure that the most suitable work systems and equipment are used, and that the whole is properly integrated with the overall management information systems. As with most things in this fast changing world, there is a continuing need to reappraise information systems and to ensure that the finer tentacles of these systems, down through a business, continue to be fully understood and effective.

Limitation

Manning standards can never be absolute because the raw material — people — varies far too much. In spite of all the political philosopy which makes assumptions that people should be treated as equal, they are not. There are obvious differences of size and strength which seem to be readily accepted, while intellectual differences which are proportionately vastly greater, are 'socially unacceptable' within the UK. I suppose that geographers faced with the Flat Earth Society a century or so ago must have felt similarly frustrated, but evidence suggests that the obvious misconceptions incorporated into political dogma will not survive indefinitely. One grieves for the harm done meanwhile.

The reality is of enormous differences between individuals which means enormous differences in the performance achievable by individuals on any type of work. Hopefully, the selection of people for any particular job will be sufficiently based on an employee specification to ensure that the group of employees can all do the work required adequately, and that individuals lacking the necessary basic abilities will have been excluded. Some reasonable average standard can be determined, excluding any exceptional performances.

Poor specification and poor selection will lead to a much wider spread of individual performances and a tendency to pull down the average standard. Efforts to raise 'quality' by setting recruitment specifications at too high a level have an equivalent impact as over-able people will become bored and frustrated, more inclined to errors, absenteeism and turnover.

3.1 Work analysis

There is a great need for the man who can be deeply involved in every aspect of work analysis. In a production unit, the work study engineer should be capable of analysing (and, if necessary, replanning) the total unit; analysing all the work done and checking why it is done; investigating materials flow and handling; establishing the individual skills required and available; and so on.

The British Standard Glossary of Terms in Work Study gives these useful definitions:

1   *Work Study* is a generic term for those techniques, particularly method study and work measurement, that are used in the examination of human work in all its contexts, and which lead systematically to the investigation of all the factors that affect the efficiency and economy of the situation being reviewed, in order to effect improvement.

2   *Method Study* is the systematic recording and critical examination of existing and proposed ways of doing work, as a means of developing and applying easier and more effective methods and reducing costs.

3   *Work Measurement* is the application of techniques designed to establish the work content of a specified task and the time for a qualified worker to carry out that job at a defined level of performance.

Work study and work measurement can be applied to almost any sort of regular operating-type work, but only with difficulty to thinking-type work. There is a requirement to be able to observe, record, and measure the actions involved in the work. The analytical work therefore tends to be a full-time job for an individual rather than a part-time job for a foreman or supervisor. This individual (the work study officer), must be continually at the location of the work under study, and able to observe and record every aspect of it with the agreement of all involved.

The more sophisticated systems provide for estimates of non-observable aspects of jobs, and various systems can be applied to cover most production, service and clerical work.

There are distinct areas of work in which we may take measurements of work fairly generally — for example, the production shop and the office — but the critical factors for selection are whether or not the work is easily observable, largely routine and operational in nature. Work of this nature lends itself readily to measurement while much administrative and non-standard technical and other activity becomes progressively more difficult to measure in a usable sense.

Now let's get down to applications.

The definition of work study quoted above showed two major aspects — method study and work measurement — which together help to improve productivity. In simple terms, method study will help to simplify each job (and perhaps to identify more economical means of getting the work done), while work measurement enables one to quantify by measuring the length of time required to do the job.

The ILO *Manual of Work Study* quotes eight steps to be taken in any work study exercise. They are:

1   Select the job or process to be studied.
2   Record from direct observation everything that happens, using the most suitable of the recording techniques available, so that the data will be in the most convenient form to be analysed.
3   Examine the recorded facts critically and challenge everything that is done, considering in turn: the purpose of the activity; the place where it is performed; the sequence in which it is done; the person who is doing it; the means by which it is done.
4   Develop the most economic method taking into account all the circumstances (method study).
5   Measure the quantity of work involved in the method selected and calculate a standard time for doing it (work measurement).
6   Define the new method and the related time so that it can always be identified.
7   Install the new method as agreed standard practice with the time allowed.
8   Maintain the new standard practice by proper central procedures.

Method study

Method study covers the first four of these steps. Early diagnosis identifies the work areas for close study.

'Record everything that happens, from direct observation', means just that. At its simplest, this could also mean *work sampling*.

In general, it is likely to be found that there is a considerable amount of slack time or ineffective work because of lack of management planning and other reasons. Some studies show effective working time as low as 25 per cent of the total. Work sampling will identify poor areas most quickly, with detailed analyses to follow. Work sampling involves making a large number of random momentary observations of either individuals or equipment, and recording what is happening at those points in time. The percentage of observations recording (say) idle men will provide a reasonably accurate guide to what is happening throughout the week (depending on the number of observations made).

This is a useful preliminary to work study proper, in that it takes far less time to cover a large area and build up a general picture of efficiency. The headings we can use for analyses of employees are: working, idle, travelling, and any other general heading that seems relevant. For example, 'fetching materials' might be significant in some areas. (For machinery, we want perhaps: working, broken down, being maintained or repaired, idle.)

Observation and recording is then extremely simple, with a tick being required against the appropriate heading for each observation. An American report states that 500 observations gives a fairly reliable result, while over 3000 is very accurate. Statistical calculation of accuracy is possible in any case, provided observations are over comparable groups or operations.

'Examine the recorded facts critically, and challenge everything . . .'

Analysis of sampling will help identify the areas for priority study. For example, some will show the sequence of events against time-scales; others will show layout and work flow. Charts of this sort must cover a considerable range of activities. Many years ago, Gilbreth invented a series of symbols to simplify charting. These symbols have been developed substantially since then, but still have the original name of 'therblig' (Gilbreth spelt backwards — almost). As examples:

O   *Operations.* This symbol is used to indicate one of the main steps in a process, method or procedure. Usually the part, material or product concerned is modified or changed during the 'operation'.

☐   *Inspection.* This symbol is used to show that an inspection for quality or quantity is made at that point.

Other symbols indicate that materials are loaded or off-loaded or moved; that there is delay; that materials are placed in stores; and so on. Many other therbligs are used in related studies; eighteen additions have been made to record micromotion studies. These include symbols for search, select, grasp, hold, assemble, etc.

Process charts using these symbols take various forms, individually
designed to enable other relevant data to be included in the record.
(Standard forms exist in many companies.)

Separate charts of one activity may show what the workers do,
what happens to material, and how the equipment is used. Rather
more sophisticated are *multiple activity* charts on which the
activities of more than one worker or machine are recorded on a
common time-scale to show the relationship between their activities.
Yet another form is charts showing the rhythm and movement of
an operator.

Inter-relationships between one activity and another, one worker
and another, and between groups of works and machines, possibly
offer the greatest scope for productivity improvement, particularly
when linked into effective work planning. Of particular relevance
is the need to plan sequencing when an activity involves varied
skills and members of different unions.

'Rhythm and symmetry' analysis can show similar opportunity for
effort and time saving. Much study of human movement in work
produced a series of obvious enough statements or rules. For example,
the hands cannot hold things and perform useful work at the same
time. Also, hands and arms should move simultaneously in opposite
directions symmetrically: and, each item must have its proper place
at the work place. Some of the more sophisticated rules that have
been developed include:

1   If the eyes are used to select material, the latter should be kept
     in the area where the eyes can see them without moving the
     head.
2   Fixtures should be provided to hold the item being worked on,
     to leave both hands free.
3   All parts should be located within the 'maximum working area',
     i.e. within reach without moving the body, and so on.

The values of these various charts become apparent when the
question 'Why?' is asked:

    Why is it done?
    Why is it necessary?
    What is actually achieved?
    What is done?
    What are the alternatives?
    What should be done?

These will draw out ideas for change and it may be found that:
'The original reason for this practice has been forgotten'. When that
happens, and there is no apparent reason for continuing the activity,
there is an immediate saving that will help productivity figures. With

the conclusion of questioning, the answers obtained should be pointing very clearly to the opportunity for 'developing the most economic method'.

3.2 Establishing manning standards

The second half of 'work study' is 'work measurement', or 'time study'. It is concerned with determining how long it takes a qualified worker to carry out a specified job at a defined level of performance. The major application is to the measurement of direct work in manufacturing areas (which we shall look at first), but the concepts are applicable to the establishment of manning standards for most types of work in all functions. (We shall go on to examine how this may be achieved.)

Time study

Time study involves the systematic assessment of the time required, thus making it possible to set time standards for work. The main application of these standards is in:
1   Planning the manning of all operations by loading individuals and machines (separately or in combination) to achievable work levels.
2   Providing a control basis, against which performance can be assessed.
3   Providing a basis for comparing efficiency of various methods.
4   Providing a basis for estimating and tendering.
    Work measurement is not a single technique, but rather a group of techniques which contribute to the applications listed. This group includes time study as its major technique, with variations and supplements such as Methods Time Measurement (MTM), synthetics and estimating.
    Time study is a technique used to determine as accurately as possible, from direct observation, the time required to carry out a given activity at a defined level of performance. Here, the time study (or work study) engineer is breaking down the activity into elements, recording the time taken for each element by the use of a stop watch and performance ratings.
    A production study extends over a long period, and is a continuous stop-watch study, often extending over one or more shifts, to check a proposed or existing time standard or to obtain other information affecting the rate of output.
    Pre-determined Motion Time Standards (PMTS) is a technique that can be used to analyse any operation into the basic motions

required to perform it. Then, pre-determined times are assigned to the motions according to the nature of the motion and the conditions under which it is made. There are a number of these systems, with time standards compiled from extensive studies. The most widely used is Methods Time Measurement (MTM). These time standards are universal, and not confined to a limited number of elements. Most production activities can be covered by this data, which also offers a useful basis for estimating time standards for production planning.

Synthetics are time standards built up from elemental times obtained earlier from direct time studies. The advantages of synthetics are similar to those of pre-determined motion time standards. Where possible, synthetics should be checked by short, direct-observation studies, to ensure that no element has been omitted.

The procedure for time study follows the same broad pattern as methods study. It is a technique for recording the times and rates of working for the elements of a job, carried out in known conditions. It is always carried out with the agreement of those concerned in the work, although this opens the way for the operator to slow down while he is being timed, which may be noticed by the work study engineer. This is particularly difficult where the standard is to be used in an incentive scheme.

The process is simple, but requires the engineer to familiarise himself with the operation first, by checking any job specification, the quality specification, any drawings in use and the tools and equipment used. He will, naturally, have been introduced to the operator concerned. Then he watches and times the operator.

He will need to watch a number of cycles of the operation, and to record both the elements and the total operation, plus performance ratings. The average of a number of cycles will be used. He should record a complete description of the methods used, broken down into the elements that he has timed, and make sure that he has recorded and timed all incidental work, such as periodic checks and adjustments to the machinery, or the time taken to clean swarf from the production area.

Ideally, the timing should be of an experienced worker, i.e. an individual with the appropriate training and skills who is experienced in the work. If a new method is introduced, any timings in the early stages are likely to be misleading as the pace of work will increase dramatically further along the learning curve.

Standards of performance may be assessed for the average experienced worker, but individual abilities vary enormously. For this reason, the observer must make an assessment of the individual's rate of working, relative to the standard rate of an experienced worker.

In the UK, a standard of 83 is used to state the standard performance, or rate of output, that experienced workers achieve as an average over a working day and with reasonable motivation. A standard of 75 is used for normal day rate and normal supervision; a standard of 100 is used where employees are motivated by incentives. The 83 is an internationally accepted MTM standard, but some other figures used in the US and in Europe are different.

These standards refer to working time, and actual averages for many departments may be substantially lower. 'Inflation' in local standards (within a factory) sometimes make a complete nonsense of these general figures. Comparison with national MTM standards is advisable when reviewing performance figures in a previously unknown factory.

As an indication of the range of individual standards, it is normal to specify within an incentive scheme that the average experienced worker can earn about a third more than basic, e.g. 100 in relation to basic 75, by achieving his expected standard performance on incentives. The effect of putting a production shop onto incentives can be to increase output by a quarter or more (but the same result might be achieved by a high day rate and improved supervision — and even better results by tackling the roots of motivation).

Standard times are calculated from observed times and observed ratings, with additions for various allowances, ranging from a personal needs allowance (to cover visits to the lavatory, etc), through a variety of work-orientated allowances for heavy work, poor light, air conditions, noise, mental strain, monotony, etc. Allowance may also be made in standard times for delays.

Relaxation allowances are an addition to the 'basic time', intended to provide the worker with the opportunity to recover from the physiological and psychological effect of carrying out specified work under specified conditions and to allow attention to personal needs. The amount of these allowances will depend on the nature of the job. Other allowances include:

Authorised breaks
Machine or tool adjustment
Rejection of defective product
Interference
Unoccupied time
Defective material
Process instability
Balance delay
Contingencies

Standard times provide the supervisor with a clear guide to the amount of work or output that he can expect, and directs him to take action if actual output is habitually short.

I made a brief mention of MTM above. MTM has become one of the advanced members of the predetermined motion-time family of systems, being very complex. Variations have been developed by various consulting firms. A feature of these systems is that they will utilise a variety of measurement techniques, ranging from time studies to special forms of photography.

These systems analyse any manual operations or methods into the basic motions required to perform them and assign predetermined time standards to each motion, based on the nature of the motion and the condition of operation.

The more sophisticated MTM-2 systems trimmed analysis time and presentation, based on the considerable volume of MTM data available.

Very much simpler is the technique developed by ICI known as Simplified PMTS, which is also motion-time measurement. It was designed for quick learning and application. Once relatively easy rules have been absorbed, MTM-type systems have some application in the use of office machinery, but are not really designed to measure clerical work.

Detailed operation of any of these systems required assistance from experienced analysts and/or consultants. However, a great deal has been published, and some degree of choice may be made by studying the literature. These systems make it possible to assess the effectiveness of clerical work performance and control this through the quality of supervision; also to tackle problems of a major review of methods.

As with work study, there may be occasions when the tightness of the controls that emerge will inhibit work satisfaction and initiative, and by these means offset part of the productivity increase obtained by the tighter controls

Application of work study principals in the office

Most work study is applied to the straightforward aspects of work, particularly machine operation, assembly operations, and in the office covering most typing activity, printing, duplication, calculating and accounting machine operations and teleprinting. Some of the main techniques of office work measurement are MTM and time study, although O&M is the general term used for office work study.

The stages of time study involving observation, timing and recording, are open to human error on a small scale, as from the beginnings of assumptions about pace of work and selection of basic times, human judgement begins to reduce objectivity. With the determination of contingency allowances and conversion to standard times, human judgement plays a major part.

There is, of course, considerable data on every aspect of this process, and well-defined norms for the various relaxation and special allowances, but it is in these areas that most conflict can arise, with opinion differences able to influence times by significant amounts. Excessive influence may be exerted either by an aggressive management negotiator, or by a similarly aggressive employee representative. In either case, the value and acceptability of the work study can be seriously affected.

Work study is basically a management aid, but it has considerable impact on the employees concerned, and there is general acceptance that participation in the study and agreement of the final result is essential. This imposes a need to be fair and logical in the entire approach. It may be naive to suggest that complete openness and honesty are required from all participants, but if bending the rules goes too far, both sides are defeated.

Best results probably require a committee acceptance, based on access to the full study data, reasonable knowledge of the whole group of jobs under study, and an open-minded approach to the views expressed by the various other participants. If the end result can be treated flexibly, so that spot studies may continue and any anomaly may be corrected, the pressures from wrong ratings may be overcome and general fairness may be observed.

Clerical work can be analysed up to a point, mainly by time study of components, but work requiring thought, or non-standard activity generally, cannot be accurately assessed. In this area, only the use of 'synthetics', which makes assumptions about average times required for volumes of a particular area of activity, could be used.

There are a variety of clerical work analysis techniques, many of which seem to be patented schemes designed by management consulting firms, but almost all of which seem to be derived from the common backgrounds of time study, PMTS, estimating and activity sampling. Thus the many different sets of initials may do little more than confuse the intending user.

The stated objectives of most schemes fit into the broad headings of providing a basis for cost control and manning standards, and providing some ground-work for methods improvement. The methods of implementation and maintenance vary to a similarly limited extent. Most require the use of trained analysts who analyse the work done with varying degrees of thoroughness and build up forms of standard times.

The purpose of these schemes is to measure the time taken to perform the work content of an activity. In each case, some assumption has to be made about the workpace (as individuals vary enormously in their abilities to do work at particular speeds).

In recent years, the systems used in sophisticated environments have tended to draw from each of the available data creation methods and synthesise time standards to standard data or synthetics.

Standard times are determined by actual observed times taken to complete specific work units. They are quoted in hours and minutes, and should represent the average of a series of separate measurements. They make no specific claim in respect of work standard achievable, but management may define performance standards expected in relation to standard times; for example, 80 per cent where 100 is the standard time as measured.

Some of the detailed systems of application are as follows:

WOFAC

This is a system patented by a consulting company which dates back to about 1938, although the system has been updated from time to time, and is currently known as VeFAC (the registered trade name for the system). The system aims at control over the work and staffing situation, partly by controlling the flow of work and relating this to staffing requirements. This it does by controlling the flow of work from the supervisor to work groups, and ensuring regular face-to-face contact between the supervisor and subordinates.

Targets are developed rather than work measurement standards, being reasonable time expectancies within which a task can expect to be completed. They are based on a combination of observation by analysts or consultants, records of activities kept by employees, and experience of supervisors. Targets are agreed between the parties concerned, and must be considered achievable by the employee concerned and his superior.

Once targets have been established, these are used as standards by a supervisor, who divides work into batches. Each batch is passed to an employee, who must return it completed before getting the next batch. Any delay beyond the target time is investigated by the supervisor.

This approach places an excellent control mechanism in the hands of the supervisor, but appears to have some of the characteristics of job fragmentation in limiting the 'independence' of the clerk or operator and the satisfaction he might have from his work. However, this must be balanced against the substantial improvement in productivity that generally results from this control.

Group Capacity Assessment (GCA)

This is also a consultant-designed system. A major feature of this system is the building of time standards for groups of employees, where possible, covering a sequence of operations. The wide variation in individual abilities is acknowledged. By 'averaging' the work of a group to produce standards in line with the group's capacity, any subsequent change in the mix of the group should not create problems of revising standards.

Standards are based on a mix of time study, a shortened form of work sampling, plus synthetics, and the estimates of skilled analysts.

Time standards are established which allow for 'normal' pace of work with allowances for fatigue, etc., and are agreed with management, but not with employees and their supervisors (although supervisors are given extensive GCA appreciation training). The supervisor is provided with the means of doing his job of controlling and maximising work flow for groups of four to twelve staff.

Abbreviated systems

There are many in-company and consultant-packaged variations on the theme of applying work study type principles to the task of establishing manning standards for indirect and similar work. The approach you choose will depend on your environment and on your preferences; and on the extent to which work *measurement* may be acceptable to the employee groups who will be involved in the studies. The range of options is opened up by our ability to make use of existing management data to develop a form of manning standards, so that at one extreme there are systems which require specialised job analysis by trained analysts who cover an average of two jobs a week; while at the other extreme are simplified forms which try to achieve a similar end result, cutting out as much expensive analysis time as possible.

These 'partial-measurement' schemes concentrate on establishing the main 'chunks' of work and the factor or factors on which variation in manning requirement depends. Starting from existing manning standards (the present, actual position), it is possible to observe variations in the utilisation of people over several weeks, with the objective of stabilising utilisation at the levels achieved in the better weeks. This approach places the responsibility for improvement very strongly with the local supervisor or manager, and in good hands can be at least as effective as more expensive systems.

The steps which can be taken along this road can be kept at a very simple level, with some benefits arising and evident from each step. The first is the preparation of an extremely useful aid to reviewing current manning – the 'span of control' chart (see Figure 3.1).

	General Accounting (A)	Cost Accounting (A)	Credit (A)	General Accounting (B)	Payroll (B)	Accounts Payable (B)	Credit (B)	Systems
LEVEL 1	Division Comptroller 5 (+2)							
LEVEL 2	Unit Comptroller 'A' 4 (+1)			Unit Comptroller 'B' 3 (+1)				Systems Manager 3 (+2)
LEVEL 3	Manager General Accounting 2 (+1)	Manager Cost Accounting 2 (+1)	Manager Credit 2 (+1)	Manager General Accounting 4 (+1)			Manager Credit 3	Senior Analyst 1
LEVEL 4	Supervisor General Accounting 6	Supervisor Payroll 2	Supervisor Credit 1	Supervisor General Accounting 10	Supervisor Payroll 2	Supervisor Accounts Payable 2	Clerical 3	
LEVEL 5	Clerical 6	Clerical 2	Clerical 1	Clerical 10	Clerical 2	Clerical 2		

Each box contains the title and the number supervised. The number in parentheses indicates non-supervisory posts

Figure 3.1 'Span of control' chart

DEPARTMENT *Finance* SECTION *Vouchers*

	Available hours	APL	MAY	JUN	JUL	AUG	SEP	OCT	NOV	DEC	JAN	FEB	Average
1	Headcount (excl)	5½	5½	5½	5½	4	4	4	4	4	4	4	
2	Headcount (incl)												
3	Contracted hours	825.00	825.00	1031.25	825	600	750	600	600	1050	450	600	
4	Overtime	28.25	3.5	8.25	3.5	–	20.75	53.75	59.25	28½	16.75	13.25	
5	Transfers in												
	Sub-total (a)	853.25	828.5	1039.5	828.5	600	770.75	653.75	659.25	1078½	468.75	613.25	
6	Holidays (annual)	3.75	203.00	69.25	116.25	153.75	236.25	36.00	7.5	142½	45	22½	
7	Sickness	88.50	129.5	15.5	7.5	5.25	7.5	97.00	87.75	58	7½	15	
8	Transfers out												
	Sub-total (b)	92.25	332.5	84.75	123.75	159.00	243.75	127.00	95.25	198½	52½	37½	
9	Net attendance	761.00	496.0	954.75	704.75	441.00	527.00	526.75	564.00	880	446.25	575.75	
10	WDF input	2160	1474	2143	1275	1154	1343	1471	1415				
11	WDF output	2096	1783	2493	952	1377	1377	1440	1424	2413	898	1760	
12	WDF balance	1110	801	451	700	551	523	574	565				
13	Activity ratio	2.8	3.6	2.6	1.4	3.1	2.6	2.7	2.5	2.7	2.1	3.1	
14	Rolling average												

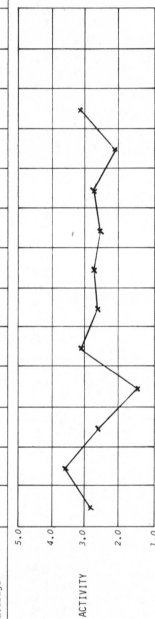

ACTIVITY

5.0
4.0
3.0
2.0
1.0

Figure 3.2 Supervisor's control chart

These charts show, for a company or division or department of up to about 1000 maximum (on one chart), the number of reporting levels and the precise span of control of each supervisor and manager. They highlight immediately any serious excess in the number of levels, either generally or in a specific department; any 1-over-1 situations, use of deputies or assistant managers; narrow spans of control which could be wider; and so on. It is an excellent aid to identifying and smoothing out anomolies in organisation structures and the excess manning invariably associated. In particular, it shows up any excess of management and supervisory positions.

From this charting, it is logical to proceed to look at all of the larger groups of manpower in more detail, reviewing with each supervisor the measures he uses privately to establish his needs for changed manning. Usually, there are factors that might be called 'work demand factors' which have been loosely identified, or may have been quantified already because they are clear cut (key punch depression rates for punch operators, or invoice rates for invoice typists).

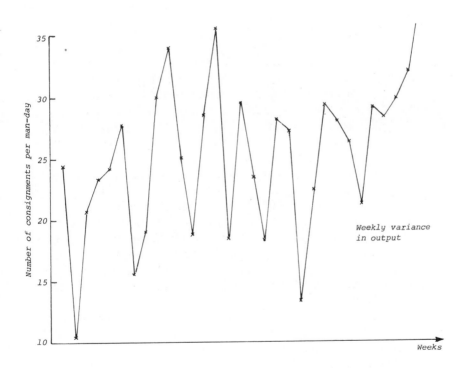

Figure 3.3 Supervisors' control chart

Supervisors are encouraged to plot on simple graphs their available manpower after allowing for absence or overtime, against their chosen work demand factor. After plotting this data for a few weeks, what does it tell them about the way they use their people? Usually, it shows widely differing levels of utilisation, week to week, and the supervisors are then encouraged to ask their own questions (see Figures 3.2 and 3.3).

Can they justify to themselves the low utilisation in some weeks, and what are they doing about it? Also, is the work demand factor meaningful, or should some other factor be sought? Enthusiastic supervisors quickly begin to set improvement targets, to smooth out manpower utilisation, and to run their departments with fewer people (achieved either by natural wastage or reduction in temporary staff).

The stage beyond this generally involves specialist help in the form of an examination of systems, of work done to ensure it is essential, of job structures to see if these can be improved, and of the manning standards evolved by the supervisor. Carefully done as the supervisors 'own study' rather than an imposed external exercise, measurement may be introduced acceptably, and the supervisors find scope for additional improvement.

The following is taken from a progress report in one company:

In current programmes, improving manpower management is an ongoing activity which involves, and is found valuable, by managers, supervisors, and foremen and is a firm basis for manpower planning. The success of these programmes over the past year rests on the extent to which supervisors and foremen have been absorbing the technique into their own activities as a valuable aid. Where support was withdrawn deliberately for several months and the only motivation to continue arose from the value felt by the supervisors themselves, several new developments and improvements were evolved, and in no case was the activity discontinued.

Management reaction to the manpower function is primarily expectation of control, (where an excess of 100 personnel for a year has a profit after tax impact of £0.25 million − 1978/79). Meaningful control needs a sound base of adequate manning guidelines for all activities, used as a basis for manpower plans, which in turn provide the base for controlling actual manning levels. Manpower management goes further and is closely related to the utilisation of people, who work more productively in suitably designed jobs, using suitably designed systems, with reasonable delegation and involvement.

Against this background, the manpower management programme sets out to ensure effective practice in setting manning standards, planning and controls, and responds to

the human needs noted subsequently, in evaluating desirability
and potential for work restructuring, in 'flagging' need for
systems changes, and deeply involving line management at all
levels in responsibility for manpower management. The response
of junior to middle management has been very encouraging and
*this group is seen as a major resource in improving our use of
people.*
In practical terms, the objectives of the current programme are:
—   To re-establish proper manning standards covering all
      indirect categories.
—   To install a simple reporting system which will give
      everybody, and particularly junior management, continuous
      information on the utilisation of manpower. (This refers
      specifically to that labour which does not produce standard
      hours.)
—   To use the system as a tool to increase the awareness of
      manpower utilisation, to ensure that it reaches and is
      maintained at satisfactory levels.
—   To provide information on current and future manning
      requirements.
The complete programme comprises seven phases, which do
not always follow the same sequence:
1   Introduction of the programme and its objectives to all
     involved.
2   Detailed analysis of the work to be done, systems in use,
     relevance of all actions involved.
3   Improvement of workflow and content, and identification
     of significant systems changes required — where appropriate.
4   The establishment of initial work standards and manning
     levels.
5   The installation of work movement and manpower
     utilisation controls.
6   The training of management and supervision in the use of
     the controls.
7   The subsequent maintenance of the system by the users.

Experiments   The work began a year ago and made some use
of earlier studies, (now outdated) but some were totally new.
It concentrated on steps 5, 6 and 7, placing emphasis on local
junior and middle management making better use of information
already available to them, to evaluate for themselves their
utilisation of people. Gradually, they began to tell us that for
the first time, they had guidelines to their own manpower
requirements.
    For subsequent periods of four to six months, they were left
alone to see whether the system would die. Without exception,

all continued in use, through periods of major change and redundancies in some areas, and with no adverse trade union reaction. Several supervisors improved the form of analysis. Vitually all took actions which improved their manning standards. All felt better informed and more able to make positive comment on manning requirements for budgeting, several volunteering targets in excess of current achievement.

It is of critical importance to note that the initiative for much improvement came from a level of management previously excluded from real involvement in manpower planning and control, and to highlight the further potential which this implies.

The current programme is flexible, but will cover the 'seven steps' working across all departments with departmental staff, to review work volume and manning requirements, to consider the effectiveness of work structuring, systems in use, need for work, implementing immediate changes required and helping supervisors and managers create their own means on monitoring subsequent manning performances.

The recognised risk of IR difficulty in this activity is minimised by open communication by involvement, and by modification to the methods used. The objective is to provide supervision with a means of monitoring their own performance and discussing this with their staff.

The relationship with the Systems functions is important and has been examined in detail. In brief, the normal approach will be that manpower analysis teams will exist at divisional level, and that general reviews of system effectiveness will be a natural by-product of their studies. (The skills required for manpower analysis and for systems development are not dissimilar, but the pace and coverage of manpower analysis will be much faster than in systems change.) Where systems change is thought necessary, this will be identified to Systems for detailed investigation and action by the most suitably experienced people.

The opportunity for involvement, and improved use of people, appear to be the critical factors which lead to support. It may be that questions of sharing advantages by means of wage and salary increase will delay some opportunities, but all evidence to date suggests that this is not likely to be a major limitation on the programme. Indeed, where work restructuring leads to improved manpower productivity, re-grading and payment changes will follow naturally.

Whatever system is used to establish manning standards, some groups will be excluded where future requirements will have to be on a judgement basis of required or not required. It is essential that all positions treated in this way should be listed, together with a brief note of the justification for exclusion, and that these lists should be under continual scrutiny to ensure that no unnecessary jobs slip through and continue their existance. Included on the list will be:

1 Managerial positions, covered and specified within the company organisation, and likely to be under continual review as organisation structures are reviewed. This will extend down to middle management positions, and possibly to most if not all supervisory positions. Span of control charts (see again Figure 3.1) are invaluable for general review of these positions, but organisation review should ensure that they are necessary, or are not; that the number of levels is appropriate and the span of control is reasonable.

Many of these positions will have secretaries. The need for all forms *personal staff* should be reviewed from time to time, ensuring the necessity — or the acceptance of 'status' appointments. High level audio pools, kept to a small size, can produce great secretarial savings.

2 Specialist departments are frequently small, and cover a varied and changing work load. These would include the central staff departments, whose objectives and manning should be evolving continually, and whose manning requirements will fluctuate and change. There is a need for continual monitoring and audit of influence, and of adapting to change.

Centralised services are not the same as central staffs (whose roles are more fluid). In general, I would expect the bulk of centralised services work to be measurable.

3 Finally, most organisations have numbers of *project and discretionary* positions, created to achieve specific and defined objectives within defined time-scales. If management define a need and accept the cost implications, our ongoing task is to ensure that the requirement for the position it maintained; and that on completion of the assignment, the positions created are discontinued. Initial studies can usually achieve a series of immediate savings by identifying project and discretionary positions which have continued indefinitely after completion of their initial purpose, and further savings from jobs created to provide data to the first group of deleted positions.

List, challenge and audit provide the basis for both determining
needs and for subsequent control.

Manning standards by functions

The factors that influence manning standards for current manufacturing activity are likely to be somewhat different from those
which determine standards for design engineers developing future
products. It is proper that we should look at the activities in
each major function separately.

As we develop standards for accounting staff in one part of the
organisation, it is likely that this data will have some relevance to
manning standards for other accounting staff groups. It is unlikely
to give us everything we need for the second situation, but as we
cover additional groups of these staff, then the extent to which
available data helps evolve standards in subsequent areas must
increase steadily. The assembly and use of all available data in
'functional pools' is therefore very important.

The short sections which follow cover some major functions and
comment on how standards may be evolved.

Manufacturing Function   Some of the data to be assembled as a
starting point would quantify the volume and mix of manufacturing
required over, say, the next twelve months. Apart from the number
of basic units planned, a full breakdown of the component parts
should be added, together with notes on what was to be made in-
house, and what purchased externally; what inspection would be
required; what industrial engineering work was involved; and so on.

The objective would be to 'flesh out' the forward organisation
structure with some detail of the work to be done, by department
and section.

Manning standards would be built up from current data, but also
on estimates of times required for new activities or activities required
in substantially changed volumes. For example, if the department
handling all incoming materials has been measured recently, but the
mix of materials is to change, it may be possible to estimate the
impact of the changed mix, and confirm this by selective re-measure-
ment later. Or it may be possible to adapt standards from another
division with comparable mix of incoming materials.

Within manufacturing, there are probably 4 to 6 major activity
groups:
   Production operations.
   Quality and inspection.
   Production scheduling, purchasing and inventory control.
   Materials handling and stock.

Industrial engineering.
Maintenance and plant services.
Manning standards can be developed within each of these and be
comparable across divisions or subsidiaries. Within each, there may
be a further half dozen sub-groupings which will command individual
standards, and be comparable across several units.

Not all jobs fit into tidy patterns. Many are individual to one
situation. A proportion of jobs always exist for some specific purpose;
will change over 2-3 years, and standards are not applicable. There will
be a need for a production manager, for both £100,000 and
£10,000,000 volumes of output — but probably not two for either
volume.

There should be a full listing of all positions outside those covered
by standards. The list should be under continual scrutiny, to ensure
that the jobs must exist and that no standards can be set.

Technical Function   Research and development activities are the
most difficult areas in which to set manning standards. Those set
invariably contain a number of individual judgements, and the same
judgements apply when monitoring the standards. (How long does
it take to think!) Even where standards are defined in some way and
appear reasonably tight, there is scope for individual interpretation.
I have seen two comparable development departments assess their
requirements for the same piece of work, using the same systems and
standards, result in one department assessing their requirement at
twice the manpower required by the other.

So first, there is a need for a tough technical man with some
practical experience of technical manning to get involved in this
specialised work. Secondly, it is essential to break down the technical
programme, project by project, into the detailed component parts;
for the requirement is to quantify the manning necessary for each
part; to build up a PERT chart to show sequencing of use of people;
to define how each project will be done through people of stated
skills. The greater part of this work cannot be measured. What we
must seek to do is to understand the steps in the programme and
gradually build up a case law on each, making assessments of work
pace and scope for faster coverage. Inenvitably, technical people vary
in skill and ability, so that pace will be very variable, but reasonable
norms can be built up and monitored by someone who is living with
the project of setting manning standards in a technical area.

The need to make comparisons between different departments,
divisions, companies, and even internationally, is important. There
is opportunity to point out variations to slack departments and
increase pressure on technical managers who regularly demand
excessive resources by other standards, in relation to output as well
as objectives. (And recognise that higher technical standards than the

product requires costs money and may give no return.)

The more routine aspects of technical department work are more amenable to measurement, and normal standards can be developed. These are likely to be easily transferable to other comparable technical departments.

Marketing Function   In sales and marketing activities where numbers are small, there will be a listing of individual and one-off jobs which you need or do not need, at managements' discretion. Only small pockets may be measurable, or may be covered by one of the abbreviated approaches.

Where the scale of marketing is larger – the numbers of people relatively more substantial – there is likely to be a great deal of scope for reviewing and establishing manning standards. I would choose to approach this function through the steps of the abbreviated system first, and identify areas most likely to benefit from detailed analysis and measurement.

The 'discretionary' posts in marketing do need continual monitoring. Marketing objectives are under continual scrutiny, and change in response to changing pressures and strategies in the market place. It is too easy to leave a job which was created to tackle a problem which ceases to be of interest, when the logical step is to stop all activity associated with the obsolete problem. Combing through the discretionary list should highlight this situation.

Personnel Function   How much activity is measurable in the personnel function? Activity such as recruitment is measurable if the volume and type of recruiting is reasonably stable, but there are difficulties in irregular areas. Most of the personnel administration area is measurable. Training can have manning standards established. Most of the rest will go on the list of jobs excluded from standards.

The concern in personnel is always to ensure that the work of the 'excluded' or discretionary jobs really is necessary. The review should seek confirmation of purpose, and pay-back on the invest-ment. If there is to be activity of a purely research nature, then it should be identified and highlighted as such.

Administration and Finance   How much of the administrative activity in local government and public services is really necessary? Probably at least half could be discontinued without any ill effect on the services. In particular, the Health Service appears so bogged down with administration that the real objectives of the service have been lost and priorities are to administration rather than health.

This is an area where lean, purposeful manning is required. Fat is frequently abundant, and must be cut out ruthlessly. There is little difficulty establishing manning standards for many of the activities, but great difficulty in gaining agreement as to what activity is essential.

Why do you do it? What is done with it? Who uses it? These are the questions. And of the users 'What would happen if you didn't get that report monthly?

The use of span of control charts and the abbreviated format are excellent starters in 'fat' areas. They tend to show organisational chaos, and blurred decision-making. If it is really bad, try to clear out the existing organisation and existing systems and redesign to meet your real needs. As I've said elsewhere, flabby manning and poor organisation only retain second-rate people. Competent, high-ability people,will have become dissatisfied with the sharing out of work and lack of real scope. Redesign to get things back on track may need some retraining and redeployment, and probably some gentle surgery.

In efficiently run finance departments, manning standards can be set for cost accounting; for ledger work; for financial accounting generally; for data processing; and these standards should be easily transferrable between divisions or subsidiaries. Either abbreviated or measurement systems can be effective.

Learning time and manning standards

Learning time needs to be taken into account in determining forward manpower requirements wherever a significant number or proportion of the working group will be under training, and performing at a level below that of the average performance of trained and experienced manpower.

The amount of allowance made depends on the length of time required to reach competent standards of performance. This is usually illustrated in graph form as a 'learning curve' (see Figure 3.4), which shows performance level against a time-scale. In the example shown, the growth in trainee learning tapers off below the average level for experienced manpower, but where past standards have been poor, it is not unusual for the learning curve to finish above the present average level.

It is important that the selection and training should be designed to bring suitable people up to competent performance in the shortest achievable time, as extended training time is costly in under-utilisation of equipment, and poor return on remuneration costs.

The times required in training vary enormously, from a few days or weeks to many months for retraining and redeployment at high skilled levels. During that time, if 'normal performance' is 100, a trainee group averaging 50 will need twice the number of people to produce the required output: but by 67 they need only 1½ times,

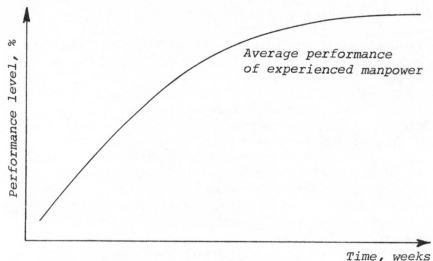

Figure 3.4 Learning curve

and by 80 only 1¼ times the number of people. Manpower planning must take these figues into account so that a balanced end result is achieved.

If turnover is high and the learning curve is long, a permanent manning level of 110-120 men may be required to cover work theoretically requiring 100, based on currently achieved performance of established personnel.

So balance is critical, and misjudgement can lead to overmanning at the end of a period of build up if retention rates are higher than expected, or the learning curve is exceeded.

An equivalent effect can result where long established, low-performance standards are suddenly raised. I know of a factory where average performance was 'stuck' below the 60 mark, but rose rapidly following a change of manager. The inevitable result was that the factory was overmanned. Rather than wait for natural wastage to correct the situation, the manager weeded out the less competent and lazy — which had the effect of further increasing the average. Apart from the obvious impact on profitability, the morale of the workforce rose sharply, and union-management relationships improved with increased respect for managerial competence.

It is important to allow for learning time in all growth or increased volume situations, and also in areas of exceptionally high employee turnover. The cost, in terms of additional manpower required, is a strong factor in encouraging reduction of turnover.

In conclusion, learning time is one more essential factor to incorporate in manpower requirement plans.

Of the various improvement ideas that emerge from method studies, some at least are likely to involve reallocation of duties and the possibility of restructuring jobs. The reasons will vary, from cold 'industrial engineering logic', to psychological reasons designed to improve individual worker motivation.

In the productivity improvement/job enrichment fields, the skills of the industrial engineer and of the psychologist are of equal importance. A major part of the industrial engineer's work of interest here is 'work structuring', defined as the 'organisation of work', the work situation and the conditions of labour in such a way that, while maintaining or improving efficiency, job content accords as closely as possible with the capabilities and ambitions of the individual employee. If this sounds also like job enrichment — it is. Job structuring may be looked on as the 'mechanics' end of enrichment, in that it is aimed at reducing the harmful effects of division of labour beyond reasonable limits, and the activity to go on under the control of or in close collaboration with a personnel specialist knowledgeable in the behavioural sciences.

Job enrichment covers this activity as a generalisation. There are a variety of forms of work restructuring that are sometimes included under this heading but have alternative names.

Enrichment generally refers specifically to the process of restructuring by dropping low-ability tasks and substituting other tasks at the same general ability level as the remainder of the job, and taken from jobs at higher levels.

One variation of job enrichment occurs where the level of work remains unchanged, but where each member of a group participates in a much wider range of activity. For example, a team of girls on an assembly line, each doing a fragmented portion of the assembly, might now be required to carry out complete assemblies with the satisfaction of producing finished articles. Although the level of satisfaction is altered enormously, the work remains essentially at the same level.

The other variation may be used where 'enlargement' seems not to be practical. Individuals are 'rotated' between the various fragmented activities with some degree of choice. Generally, most participants have a marginal preference for one or other of the 'fragments' and the group settles into a situation of chosen jobs.

To go back a stage, to the earlier principle of simplifying jobs — the engineer aimed at the simplest possible work unit with the minimum training period and maximum ease of replacement. A small number of longer-service workers would acquire greater flexibility to 'fill in'. Training and replacement costs of personnel were therefore low.

The industrial engineer accepts a high price for this ease and low cost of manning. Work-in-progress tends to be high; quality relatively poor and scrap rates expensive; feedback on faults to workers tends to be poor or non-existent; work demands are low and concentration almost negligible.

By restructuring, job cycles of very short duration such as a few seconds are replaced with longer sequences. It appears that the longer the cycle (subject to the capability of the individual) the more positive is the attitude to the work, the better the response to change and the higher the rate of working. A significant part of the apparent improvement in productivity results from cutting out the many actions of passing work to the next operator. Also the volume of work-in-progress is cut dramatically.

Although these improvements show real cost savings, the implementation cost may be high. Additional training is required, re-layout of production units, some additional or changed equipment and initially a lower pace of work until the employees are sufficiently familiar with the type of work. As learning curves show, the initial rate of improvement is slow, then speeds up as individuals get the feel of the work, and then tapers off to slow improvement over a long period. (With the single fragments of work repeated hundreds of times, the learning time to proficiency is considerably shorter than in enlarged jobs.)

Supervisory jobs are also influenced by this process, as a part of the supervisory process of work allocation disappears, and detailed supervision becomes less necessary in the enriched areas. A small number of supervisors spend more time on forward planning and being consulted by subordinates in need of help. Retraining of supervisors is critically important and may be covered by an industrial engineer/training officer working in the field, as well as the classroom.

A 'second generation' phase follows on for the behavioural scientist/industrial engineer team, once enrichment and enlargement are well developed. Just as the supervisory jobs are altered and reduced in numbers, so they absorb much of the ancillary work done for the production department. Separate activities such as planning and scheduling, inspection and quality assurance can be decimated because the production units are naturally doing all this themselves, and require only general co-ordination. Manpower savings in overall restructuring now become significant, and lines of communication become shorter and more efficient.

3.4   Inertia of existing standards — attitudes to change

Very few manning requirements are examined against a blank background. Even if the organisation is new, there will normally be a pattern of industry, or regional practice, which immediately imposes some restriction. Almost always, there exists some history of stated workload requiring a known number of people.

These past standards may have evolved from indifferent or incompetent use of financial and manning control mechanisms. Often the only factors used to develop crude departmental budgets were the figures which applied in the previous year, with *ad hoc* judgements on necessary changes and pious hopes for an 'about right' result.

A product of this vague approach, and of other contributory factors, is that manpower levels have often been allowed to ride too high. New machinery in the factory, for example, might have increased productivity, yet redundancy tended to be avoided. 'Useful' employees were stock-piled against vague future needs, or excessive manning was negotiated by a union fearful of redundancy. Through this action, and from employees' natural instincts to justify their employment, work was carefully shared, or fenced off into separate compartments for protection, so that restrictive practices built up. We all know the results of this sort of thing — retaining mates for craftsmen; demarcation disputes, with their wide variation in borderlines from plant to plant; regular overtime arrangements to maintain income regardless of work needs; and so on.

The result of these past actions is that we now have widespread under-utilisation of labour in this country — and widespread acceptance of the fact.

Productivity improvement invariably involves changing attitudes and training in new skills at supervisory and junior to middle management levels. The reasons why productivity is at current levels, is generally because the existing managers do not know how to improve. Show them the means and help them patiently, and the improvements will come.

> In a construction company, I reported that productivity at site level was very low due to poor planning site layout, materials handling and manpower utilisation and suggested that a general improvement of 20 per cent or more seemed completely feasible.
>
> The managing director concerned pulled a report from his desk dated ten years earlier, saying that he knew about these things, but what should he do. The things he had tried had produced no result.
>
> The problem was tackled by training the contracts management in the various skills required. This was followed by training site agents and foremen on site in the routines they should follow to tighten their own working disciplines. By increasing their knowledge of how to plan and control every aspect of their work, and by helping them practically during

the initial work, we reached the stage where they suddenly realised that life was less stressful and the contracts were going easier.

Back in his office, the managing director watched the performance figures begin to rise, and go up far more than he had hoped for as the planning and control spread naturally into every other aspect of his business over a two-year period.

Changing the existing pattern on purely logical grounds may be totally unacceptable to the employees affected, yet change without their support is not practicable. So, any change in accepted standards must be on a basis acceptable to both employer and employees; and each must feel it to their own advantage. There is no standard cost formula or balance to be achieved, but the new arrangements must seem reasonable to those affected.

In obtaining agreement to changes, a number of factors are relevant:

1   Management must understand and support the proposed changes and the reasons for them.
2   Employees must be satisfied that they will be treated fairly, and that the end results will be acceptable to all those affected, both directly and indirectly.
3   The agreement, when made, must be sufficiently clear-cut to ensure points of detail are not subsequently disputed.

Management support stems from a thorough analysis of the situation under review which enables the whole picture and proposal to be clearly communicated to managers. If the purpose and objectives are understood and potential benefits can be appreciated, then positive management encouragement and support for change — for improvement — will result, and management enthusiasm will be communicated naturally to those of their staff who may be affected.

The prime objective is to obtain the support of the individuals affected. A great deal can be achieved, assuming the proposal is sound, through the informal relationships that exist between managers or supervisors, and the employees affected. Where employees have natural or elected leaders as spokesmen, such as shop stewards or staff committee representatives, a second level of support must be obtained. Where trade unions are involved, a third level of agreement with district or national officials may be necessary. The influence of the second and third levels may be no more than marginal if the proposal is shown to be acceptable to the individual employee.

The key is acceptability of proposals. We thus need to examine the sort of points on which employees must be satisfied. These appear to be primarily economic, but the proposal must not seem inequitable, or significantly worsen security of employment.

The economic aspect is straightforward. If a proposed change (in working arrangements) will alter earnings potential, some compensatory adjustment will be expected in order to maintain earnings levels. For example, if systematic non-essential overtime is to be discontinued, some compensatory wage or salary adjustment to maintain earnings level will be expected. Unless this is done, termination levels will rise substantially, or more drastic action may be taken as the employees will feel unfairly deprived of earning potential.

Reassurance seems necessary in respect of security. Straight redundancy associated with a proposal is assessable and becomes a factor in the bargaining. Possible future redundancy as a consequence of the short-term proposal is much less easy to assess, and some form of longer-term reassurance may be required.

If employees can be satisfied on all points under these headings, there is a sound basis for agreeing changes in staffing standards. Whether the cost to the company of change justifies the end is for the company to determine, but change will often be linked with other moves to raise productivity and offset any additional costs.

3.5 Improving manpower utilisation

The quality of our workforce determines the level at which we can set company objectives and the probabilities of success in achieving those objectives. This quality can be reduced in effectiveness by poor organisation, poor structuring of work and poor utilisation of the people we have. The central purpose of manpower planning and control is to improve utilisation of the company manpower resources.

A theme for consideration is that we must aim to move beyond control of headcount, firstly by decentralising the control to divisions where clear manning standards exist, and by delegating responsibilties for manning standards to managers and supervisors. We can then alter the control from headcount to total remuneration, giving managers greater freedom to increase manpower quality, using fewer people at higher pay levels.

As we move further to concentrate on effective manning and improving our use of the people we have, our concern for ratios should diminish as these will show steady improvement. Improving manning standards is improving use of the manpower resource.

International manning comparisons generally show UK manning standards to be very poor. While many examples prove the point, it is relevant to record that these comparisons are very difficult to make as they are complicated by differences in levels of capital investment which can have a substantial impact on manpower requirements. This should not be used as justification, as UK manning standards are very poor by international standards.

Some attitudes are quite extreme on this subject, claiming that everyone has the right to work, and that large organisations have a function of distributing money to their allocation of 'employees' (for whom there may be no work). This justification for excess manning (and no unemployment) seems to me to require political impositions — or is otherwise unacceptable to any employer. I believe that every employer has a responsibility for employing the people it needs to do the work it requires; that employers should not take up manpower resources which are not essential; that employers have a responsibility to make the best possible use of their employees.

If we need any motivation to improve utilisation, surely the rates of wage and salary inflation experienced in recent years provide this. Improved use does not involve over-working employees, or cutting out necessary activities: it does involve knowing as accurately as possible how many people are required to do the necessary work.

What is productivity?

Productivity is a measure of efficiency; a ratio between output and input. There is no standard basis of calculation or scale on which productivity may be measured in different situations. Rather, it is a general heading used to cover the widely varied forms of measurement in different industries and by different types of people.

The most general use is in manufacturing and relates the volume of output to input, where input is restricted, to input of labour. The output figure may be measured in physical units of some form, or value. In either case, changes in the form of the production units can alter the base line. Similarly, labour may be measured by numbers of people or costs; but where the mix of types of employee within the numbers can alter significantly, or wage inflation is significant, the base line is affected.

The main difficulty is that the interpretation of productivity is inconsistent and diverse. Productivity writings contain endless definitions and explanations. A brief examination of some of these points of view may help our task.

The accountant views productivity in essentially financial terms, particularly related to costing and budgeting control systems, and ratios such as return on capital employed or assets.

The personnel manager wants measures of the efficiency of people, and may use work measurement techniques to obtain figures. In the in-company situation, this can be extremely valuable data in pointing out scope for improvement and identifying the areas to tackle. The personnel manager also has a considerable need to relate the volume of manpower used to level off output, as no matter what proportion of time is properly used, this does not provide an indication of pace, and therefore of real productivity.

The work study engineer or office systems analyst also wants measures of the efficiency of people, as well as of the methods and systems they use. Their analyses may highlight the proportion of working time that is spent on achieving useful work (sometimes as low as 25 per cent) and what happens to the remaining time.

The technical man tends to seek measures of use of resources, generally excluding manpower and cash resources and concentrating on physical assets. He will want quantitative measures of many things and may overlook their relevance to the overall problems of productivity. In particular, he may ignore financial implications and motivational factors.

Quantitative measures of production times, labour requirements, material requirements and waste levels, space and machine utilisation, and so on, will intrigue him.

'It may be uneconomic to seek the minimum expenditure in the use of manpower if this detracts from the optimum use of expensive capital equipment. The combination of capital and labour can be varied to give the same output.'

Utilisation studies by engineers occasionally throw up major problems of inadequate use of expensive capital equipment, such as where heavy equipment is used at full capacity for only a fraction of the time, and overall utilisation averages below 60 per cent.

The managing director seeks indices that override any purely functional measure and guide him to action that can increase both control and profitability and gives a clear picture of activity in the various areas of his business. Oversimplified, his job is to obtain the maximum earnings from his company's activities. In this he endeavours to increase the added value of materials passing through his unit, at lowest reasonable cost (again an oversimplification). He uses a number of 'measures of effectiveness' to monitor his progress. For example:

'A plain bar of iron is worth $5. This same bar of iron, when made into horse shoes, is worth $10.50. If made into needles, it is worth $4285. If turned into balance wheels for watches, it becomes worth $250,000.' *(Murray-Ohio Corporation).*

Management is getting results through people. If a manager has more work to do than he can carry out personally, he gets it done by others: he manages. Management involves getting others to work for you, and to work effectively. For many reasons, subordinates may not work as effectively as they might. The job of improving effectiveness is the manager's, and he cannot delegate this responsibility. It is how he manages that counts.

The use of resources under the manager's control can be examined under the following headings:

1   Manpower
2   Plant and Machinery
3   Materials

— but it is the first of these that concerns us here.

An employee is expected to be at his place of work for a stated number of hours per day, week or month. How much of that time he works, and what proportion of that time is productive work is largely dependent upon the way he is managed and motivated.

Many studies have been made of how people use their working time, covering most countries of the world. These show that effective working times may frequently be as low as 25 per cent of the total, while non-productive time because of poor management may rise to well in excess of 50 per cent. It is here that we locate one of the highest potential areas for productivity improvement. Figure 3.5 shows a breakdown of the working day of an operator in a manufacturing plant. The same form of analysis would apply in many other jobs and areas, including particularly white collar and 'indirect' workers.

A part of his day is spent on fully productive work. This proportion can be measured, and the objective will be to raise this percentage as high as possible. Levels above 90 per cent are achievable; but so are figures in the 20 per cent area. To achieve the objective, it is necessary to know what happens to the remainder of his time.

Unnecessary work.   For a further proportion of the day, the employee is working , but for various reasons the work he does is unnecessary. There may be a hundred reasons for this which may not be apparent to, or under the control of the employee or his immediate superior. Some which may occur in a manufacturing area are as follows:

1   Specifications used for many of the component parts of the product may be excessively tight, involving additional work time. In many ways, the product design may add unnecessarily to manufacturing time. Within a group of related products, opportunities for standardisation for components may have been ignored.

2   Unnecessary work results from poor production facilities. If the 'ideal' machine is not available, work may take three times as long on the alternative. Wrong or poorly maintained tools may have to be used, doubling or quadrupling the time and effort required to complete a job.

3   The operator himself may not have been adequately trained. He may use poor working methods. This may be attributable to the inexperience of the foreman as well as the operator, or to the foreman's inability to communicate and instruct.

4   Production conditions such as lighting and space may be poor, and the layout of machinery and feed of materials may cause

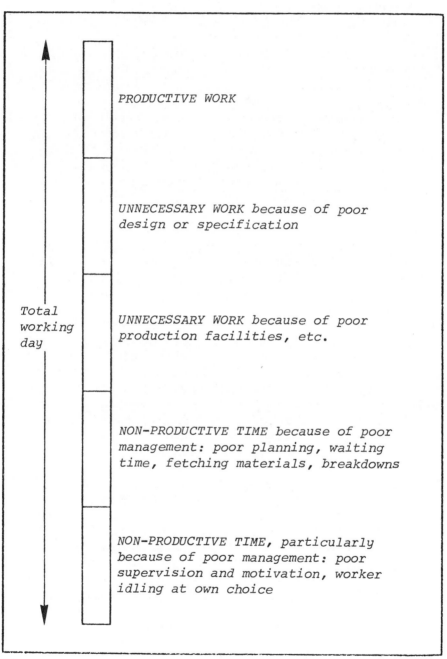

Figure 3.5 Breakdown of operator's working day

excessive or uncomfortable movement. The work pace that the individual feels able to maintain may fall rapidly in these types of situations.

Comparable situations will be found in other functions, and particularly in many indirect areas.

Non-productive time   Most non-productive time is caused by poor management in some way or other, although it is the worker who controls the amount of time he is absent from his work or idle, unless supervision is responsive.

Before being taken round a plant recently, I was offered £25 if I saw anybody stop work for longer than twenty seconds for any reason. Aggressive supervision and high rates meant that I did not get the money, but I did note misuse of time. Materials handling and storage were poor, with several separate movements being involved to get materials to the point of use, which served as an extremely time-absorbing activity.

Some of the worst examples of poor planning of materials flow that I have seen occurred on building sites where materials were always in the way of work scheduled for tomorrow, and seemed to get transported to be in the way of work scheduled for the following day, or the bricks required were at the far end of the site. Some factories seem to work on the same principle.

Bad planning can take many different forms, and in all its forms is the major factor in non-productive time which must be charged against management. Inadequate production scheduling of work results in idle time for men (and machines), and much further time is lost by shortcomings in the supply of materials to manufacturing points.

Planned maintenance helps to control and minimise idle time on machines, but if the system is not thorough enough and the plant is badly run down or antiquated, the volume of breakdowns may cause further idle time.

Another form of bad planning arises from poor marketing fore-casts and policies, with excessive product variations where these lead to short production runs and the inevitable idle time for both operators and machines due to the frequency of resetting, etc. Over-frequent design changes also slow production effort and output during pre-production experimental runs and until the changed product and its manufacture have been properly 'debugged'.

Inadequate attention to working conditions can affect productive time as excessive heat or poor light may force employees to take rest periods. They may be a contributory cause to accidents, which in turn reduce working time. (However, accidents are not always the result of any management shortcomings.)

A serious waste of time and material, manpower and machine resources arises from high scrap rates, attributable primarily to poor management.

Finally, there is the loss of time directly attributable to the
employee in the form of lateness, idleness at the job and absenteeism.
Absenteeism and lateness can play havoc with work loading and
scheduling; in fact, absenteeism in excess of 20 per cent is enough to
stop some mass-production lines.

Here, we are looking for scope in improving our use of people,
and our manning standards, rather than the other aspects of productivity improvement. The brief sections which follow give pointers to
some fruitful areas for study.

1   Systems   The systems we use to get work done will vary in
efficiency. Hopefully, the original design is done by competent
people and achieves the required results with minimum effort. A
few years later, a changing business operation continuing to use the
original system may find it has become very inefficient, with
substantial amounts on no-longer-required work still being churned
out.

The analysis that goes into establishing or updating manning
standards should automatically review the need for work being
done and review the adequacy of the system. Any change required
in the system would not be done by the manpower analyst, but
from his training he should be able to outline the new system
requirement for the department concerned and the systems specialist. Subsequently, he should monitor the impact on manning of the
systems change.

The objective here is to avoid unnecessary work, not just because
it is pointless, but because the people doing it will become aware
that their work is pointless as no-one makes any use of it. Knowledge
of that fact brings infectious frustration and adversely affects the
overall operation of the department.

2   Organisation   Analysis of organisation sometimes shows over-
detailed subdivision of activity into specialised components of one
or two people. Workload variations of 10 or 20 per cent have little
impact on manning levels, for at what stage do you double the
manning of a unit of one! Usually, the individuals concerned are in
various stages of under or overwork with no fine tuning possible.

Where it is possible to merge a number of these units into larger
groups of five or more people on work which is related, the
possibility of flexing manning with workload is immediately eased.
If only one of the earlier units is under pressure, the surrounding
ones can now, more easily, take up some of the overload.

The value of this approach clearly eases the determination of
appropriate manning, but also reduces the stress on individuals
at times of overload, giving them evidence of support in a team
situation, without taking away their original responsibility for a
specific activity.

3 *Organisation — spans of control*   As a part of periodic analysis of your organisation structure, draw out a complete picture of the number of levels you have and the spans of control of each manager and supervisor. Figure 3.2 shows a summary of such an analysis in clear and simple form.

Make sure you record the real picture, with any one-over-one relationships, and the deputies, assistants and others who have slipped into the chain. Your objective should be to achieve a balance between two factors:

1   To work with the minimum number of levels between top and bottom in order to speed communications and ensure everyone in the chain has a clear responsibility.
2   To keep spans of control manageable, taking into account the ranges of activity covered and geographic spread.

I shall not give any recommended numbers for either of these factors. They could only mislead. Rather examine your own situations and challenge the judgements that have been made. You will know what is workable; what is efficient; what is likely to be most satisfying for the people concerned.

4 *Restructuring of work*   In situations of change, the allocation and grouping of 'pieces' of work may not always be ideal. A periodic review of manning provides an opportunity to look at the structuring of work and, without necessarily altering any systems, to amend the structuring to make the best of the skills available.

One situation that frequently arises is that one special skill used in a department is in generally short supply. The personnel department is continually trying to recruit. Yet job analysis reveals that the three people in the department who possess the skill in question each use it for only 20 per cent of their working time. Any one of them, devoting half his time to using the skill could meet all the requirements of the department. It is logical to restructure work to overcome any suggestion of shortage of the relevant skill, and frequently more satisfying to the individuals involved.

The potential for improving utilisation of our manpower and generally improving manning standards is quite enormous. Probably the best source of change is through managers and supervisors being encouraged and helped to initiate change within their own departments — as set out in a short case study at the end of this chapter.

5 *Change*   Any major change provides an opening for reviewing past utilisation, to ensure as far as is practicable that the design of a fresh organisation and the manning structure are as good as present knowledge permits.

If decentralisation has been followed extensively, and we have become aware that many small accounts activities have led to

duplication in the interests of 'independence', do we take the
opportunity to centralise some of the accounting services to create
a more economic operation with wider ranging (and therefore,
potentially more satisfying) jobs?

6   *Utilisation of technical staff*   A regular complaint of technical
graduates is that their skills are not properly used; that they are used
on non-essential work; that the volume of administrative work is
excessive or could be done by clerical help.
   There have been a number of studies published which show this
sort of picture and it is easy enough to check out in your own
organisation. We followed up our analyses with detailed job analysis
and restructuring in selected departments, with the objective of
creating full technical development roles for our engineers and
having all other work covered by technical assistants and clerical
support. The results did not go smoothly. We had overdone, it
seemed, the concentration on full use of skills for our qualified
engineers. Experimentation over several months in close working
with the engineers established that they were content to spend up
to around 85 per cent of their time only on the activities they had
claimed originally were all important. But they enjoyed the 'fringe
benefit' of visits to outside suppliers of possible components and
other off-site, on-expenses activity and insisted that these were
essential parts of their jobs.

7   *Utilisation of salesmen*   We employ salesmen to sell; to bring
in orders for our products. Yet many spend a very high proportion
of their working lives driving cars and engaged in trivial 'social'
activity which has little or no impact on sales. Close analysis of
a salesman's use of time and his effectiveness can identify scope for
substantial improvement in many cases, directing effort to the more
important customers and the better prospects; improving route
planning to minimise driving time; increasing use of telephone where
face-to-face selling is not essential; and so on.

8   *Industrial relations and utilisation*   My final point is brief
although the actions involved may take a long time. In a situation
with an established pattern of poor industrial relations and many
restrictive practices, it is usual to find a combination of overmanning
(sometimes extreme), systematic overtime and low pay. Improvement
is not easy since a major change of attitudes of all involved is
required – more than just change of system – but the potential
rewards for all concerned are high.

9   *Capital expenditure on new plant* frequently leads to significant
increase in output per man, and sometimes generates demand for

increased pay on the grounds that the people are producing more.

This is false logic and must be examined carefully. The major assumption made in our pay structure is that higher levels of pay are associated with the use of higher levels of skill. So what are we to do where the achievement of increased productivity arising from substantial expenditure on new equipment *also* deskills the work. This happens frequently where processes are automated, and the new equipment requires fewer people and at lower skill levels. In this situation, it is dangerous to retain highly skilled manpower, bribed by higher pay levels to do unsatisfying low skilled work, for only industrial unrest can come from this situation.

Participation   It is my experience that improvements are unlikely to happen unless carried out with the real involvement of the supervisors and employees concerned, either formally with trade unions, or informally with the people directly; and not just with the analysis but also in the conclusions. It is, after all, those people who will be expected to make new standards work, and this is only likely if the standards are felt to be theirs.

Further, it is a curious phenomenon, but there is almost a challenge to beat 'your own standards' which is never evident with imposed levels. I have seen surprising improvements generated after conclusion of a study which recommended what appeared to be really tight manning levels. These indicate the potential in very many manning situations if the employees become motivated to achieve. Even today, this can happen without money being mentioned and good old-fashioned job satifaction re-establishes its importance.

The changes developed by the employees in some of the cases referred to in the previous paragraph came largely from restructuring work. If you change the volume, type or mix of work in a depart-ment, the logical grouping of job 'pieces' may change also. Before finalising a new series of defined jobs, it is worth taking into account the abilities and preferences of the people who will be doing the work. The extent to which work requirements and individual preferences can be matched may have a considerable impact on both manning standards and real efficiency.

There is considerable difference in the quality and pace of individuals at work, which is definitely not improved solely by upgrading the quality of manpower. In many cases, the reverse can be true. Wherever there is a volume of continuous or repetitive work which cannot be automated, it is worth down-rating manning specifications to get as close as possible to the level of intellect and personality which will be reasonably content with the work level. If the ability levels of the incumbents are too high, both pace of work and accuracy will deteriorate, absenteeism and turnover will

increase, industrial unrest will be greater, and *cost of operation will*
be massively higher.

At all levels, this becomes a factor where change of work leads to restatement of manning requirements. 'Packages' of lower-level work may need to be created to keep a smaller number of existing jobs at the old work level, and change of staffing be used to relate the new job specifications to suitable employees.

In many manning standard studies, re-grouping of job content into more acceptable packages has an immediate impact on absenteeism and turnover, so that the number of man-hours available from the existing experienced staff is immediately increased, and the actual manning standards can be improved steadily.

MANPOWER REQUIREMENT PLANNING

───────────────────────────────────

What manpower do we require to do the work which has to be done next month — next year — in five years time? The detailed answers to these questions form our manpower requirement plans.

4.1 Introduction

Manpower planning follows on from, and is complementary to, organisation planning. In other words, it is concerned with the future manning of planned and evolutionary organisation structures. This obviously covers vastly more than simply planning the future management requirements of the company, and falls into two stages.

The first is concerned with the detailed planning of manpower requirements for all types and levels of employees throughout the period of the plan. The second stage is concerned with planning of manpower supplies, to provide the organisation with the right types of people from all sources to meet the planned requirements. This second aspect leads on to the problems of individual career planning covered in the following chapter.

We have already discussed, to some extent, the basis of planning. We are concerned with making a complete analysis of future manning requirements from the organisation plans. By making a comparison with our manpower inventory, and after giving thought to factors such as individual development and termination levels, it becomes possible to calculate a balance of personnel required, who are not available internally.

The quality of manpower requirement plans depend on many

factors. There are two areas of particular importance:

1   The quality of data on current and planned future business
     volumes and mix; together with the quality of data used
     in the business plan generally on changing technology and
     markets; changed manufacturing requirements; changed
     administrative systems; and so on. If the quality of the input
     and of the subsequent analyses and assumptions has been high,
     then the general translation of this base into manpower
     requirements can be equally high — subject to

2   The quality of data on current manpower and on the use of
     that manpower; on the skills available; on loss rates; on
     promotability; on the local manpower market. If the quality of
     this data is also of a high order, then the probability of accurate
     manpower requirement forecasting is about as high as we can
     get it.

In summary, this is a quality problem, with the accuracy of the
end result dependent on the quality of the input data and subsequent
analyses and assumptions — and with the errors cumulative on a
month to month, year to year basis.

From experience, where input is of high quality, the factor most
likely to be wrong in the assumptions will be the timing of
anticipated future events. This need not be too serious. The key
aspect is that the future events have been identified, and that
planning the action required to deal with the events has taken place.
As the plan unfolds, the likely change in timing will become evident
and the plan adjusted accordingly. Only in the event of necessary
lead times of action being overtaken by dramatic changes will the
plan have an element of failure.

The manpower requirement plans a 'translation' of the business
plan, and is directly integrated with it, changing as business plan
assumptions change. If the two should ever become separated and
either part 'set in concrete' (even for a period of a year), then that
part — or the whole plan — becomes a liability rather than an aid
to efficient management.

For example, if a manpower plan assumes a level of work, but
amendments to the short-term part of the business plan show a
lesser volume of orders and therefore work required, it becomes
essential that the short-term manpower plan responds to the change —
to restrict recruitment — to plan redundancies — to carry excess
manpower for a planned period. There is a requirement for management action which must be taken in relation to the manpower
requirement plan, and not in isolation.

What are the particular advantages of manpower requirement
planning? In brief, it is the 'trigger' mechanism in our manpower
planning sequence, leading on to other phases:

1   Manning standards; ensuring that the input to requirement

planning is as good as we can get.

2 Manpower utilisation improvement; ensuring that we are doing everything practicable to improve the use of the people we have.

3 Manpower inventory; ensuring that we have a comprehensive analysis of our stock, and how it may change, both in the development of existing people, and after allowing for natural losses of people; the need for 'reducing inventory'.

4 Manpower supply; the extent to which we can meet our requirements from internal sources:
   a the plans required to meet requirements from external sources;
   b the plans to reverse supply for some categories by retraining, redevelopment, or redundancies.

These phases will lead us through a manpower plan summary, showing in detail the requirement plan over a period of time and all the actions planned to ensure our requirements are met at the appropriate times.

Company X, a company in a processing industry, planned a build-up of their electronics division; they had already carried out a market survey and knew the sales potential of their embryo new product. They prepared a detailed business plan which took fully into account the potential growth of sales and pace of technical development, drew up an organisation plan based on the business plan, and then examined their manpower requirements in detail. From the staffing point of view, there was a series of stages to go through:

1 They must build up their technical development team to increase their rate of research on the product and, by using outside agencies, further examine its market ability.

2 As the technical team produces results they must have a production-engineering team building up behind to plan the production side, to carry out trial production runs and prove that production methods are effective and prepare the equipment of a factory.

3 In due course the factory will require staffing.

4 As the factory moves towards the point of being productive, they will need marketing staff; initially, marketing planning and advertising personnel and a probe sales team, and subsequently an effective field sales force.

5 At an early stage, they will require a sharp increase in their personnel staff, and subsequently a gradual build-up of administrative staff of all types and levels to support the growth of other functions.

This outline plan provided a first stage towards a detailed manpower requirement plan showing, on a month-by-month basis,

Table 4.1 Manpower requirement: summary of monthly staff required in each position in a rapidly growing unit

Month	Management	Technical staff		Production staff			Marketing staff		Services	
		Research	Product development	Product engineering	Product direct	Other	Marketing development	Sales	Finance	Personnel
Present	1	10	—	2	—	—	3	—	2	—
1	1	10	—	2	—	1	3	—	2	—
2										
3			1							
4			4	3	1					
5										
6			6							
7									3	1
8				5	4	2		1		
9					6					
10										
11										
12										
1	1	10	8	6	8	4	3	2	4	1
2					10			3	5	2
3					12					
4					14					
5					16					
6										
7		>7	12	8		6		6	6	
8								9		
9										
10										
11		>5								
12	1		15	10		6	3	12	7	3

the numbers of people required in each category. Part of the actual analysis first prepared is shown in Table 4.1. From this chart, which shows the build-up of senior staff, it can be seen that this growth was controlled and prepared for, was known to be economically viable and could be met by planned recruitment activity.

Curiously, in this company, all non-managerial manpower requirements were forecast with much less accuracy, managers and supervisors being permitted to recruit, *ad hoc,* those employees 'they could justify'. Not surprisingly, certain problems arose, and the revised forecast at the end of the year took into account requirements for all types of personnel on a more detailed basis. In parallel, more comprehensive costing and budgeting were also introduced.

The prime lesson is that careful initial analysis provides a sound foundation for manpower planning and subsequent implementation, while omissions from the plan will come to the surface as problems.

Implementation

As the requirement plan is based on the business plan, I like to have a comprehensive extract of relevant points for application to the existing manpower base. This would include:

1   All assumptions made, as these provide the correct point from which to identify potential variances.
2   All data relevant to manpower needs or likely to affect manning requirements in any way. This could include planned capital expenditure or planned systems studies, for example. I would seek out influences which might affect the type or categories of people required, as well as those affecting total numbers.
3   All indicators of timing changes.
4   All strongly anticipated variables and planned 'flexing' from the main plan.

In parallel, I seek as detailed an analysis of current manpower and manning standards as is available. This analysis would be by employee categories.

4.2   Requirement planning based on standards

The manning requirements of each function have to be planned separately, as any global figures would be completely blurred by the different factors applying to the individual functions. Further, each function must be analysed and planned by a whole range of separate categories and levels so that the final analysis is really meaningful and provides a basis for precise action. The range of categories must include all the specific skills we use plus any new requirements for future activities.

In the previous chapter we ran through the approaches to be used for developing standards in the major functions. In the sections which follow, we examine the application of standards to determining manning requirements in each function.

Manufacturing function

As with establishing manning standards, we shall need a detailed picture of planned manufacturing activities in order to build up our manufacturing manpower requirements. We need:

1   A complete analysis of the planned manufacturing programme, 'exploding' the output expressed in major units into the details of components; divided into own manufacture and bought-in; showing the extent of assembly work; and so on.
2   Statements of established time and manning standards for all activities.

From these, a precise picture can be built up of all the direct work to be done and the time required to do it in standard hours, sub-divided by the various skill categories involved. The manpower requirement for direct manpower producing standard hours falls out as a simple arithmetic calculation.

The second group to tackle consists of all manpower directly associated with production, but not measured on as precise a basis as standard hours, and covering purchasing, stores, material handling, despatch, inspection and testing, production cost control, and perhaps the supervisory structure.

Here the same basic data on products to be manufactured can be used in relation to established manning standards for all the work groups. Ideally, the factors related to work volume around which manning levels should be flexed will have been identified for all groups, so that the calculation of precise requirements is reasonably straightforward. For example, a smaller production volume may involve a wider range of products and require a larger number of smaller volume purchase orders. This may result in an increased requirement for purchasing staff, while the same situation reduces the requirement for inspection and inspectors.

The third area in manufacture covers the indirect categories including all manpower whose work is not directly related to production requirements. These groups are more remote from the manufacturing process and less affected by variation in volumes or mix of production. However, much of the work is adequately measurable, or can be covered by an abbreviated form of manpower standard setting. Work volume related factors will exist from which to establish manning requirements against the defined levels of activity.

It is worth noting here that a variation of more than plus or minus 20 per cent from the base volume used to establish manning standards for any activity, should lead us to re-examine the standards. The work volume related factors originally used can generally be trusted up to about 20 per cent variation (sometimes more) but some doubt must occur. Further, the structure of the work group may be affected to a greater extent than could have been foreseen from a theoretical assumption about the impact of changed volume.

The last stage is to assemble the list of positions outside the categories covered by the standards we are using, and including all 'discretionary' positions planned to cover special, short-term objectives.

From analyses of the types indicated, we should be able to assemble detailed statements of manning requirements at specific points in time for several years into the future. Against each statement, we have detailed sets of assumptions, so that in the event of modification of manufacturing volume and mix plans, it is reasonably simple to re-cast the schedules and re-state the future manning requirements in full detail.

Technical function

As I discussed when we looked at the problems of establishing manning standards in research and development areas, this is the most difficult function to get right. The need to smooth out variations in judgement standards between R&D managers and determine reasonable standards requires someone to live with the problems and build up extensive case law.

The principles to be followed are straightforward enough. There will be a programme of projects to be carried out, and the technical function will have made an analysis of each one to assess the work to be done on each project against a standard series of headings, covering all the different types and levels of activity involved in the project. Some form of standard, linked to the category of manpower to be used, should be available for all activities, so that a comprehensive assessment of the types and numbers of manpower required can be accumulated. Within the analysis will be PERT charts to provisionally allocate types of individuals with defined skills, to ensure utilisation throughout a period of time, rather than assume availability of any skill and level at any time.

In theory, this approach should produce clear statements of manning requirements against reasonable standards. It fails on two counts. The first is that the standards themselves are notoriously difficult to keep lean in R&D areas — and the system used provides remarkably effective defence. The quality of the investment in reviewing standards may be the key to this problem.

The second limitation in this analysis is that it tends to be made against existing structures, manpower and use of manpower, while a more innovative approach may give a dramatically different answer. For example, if the new range of projects are showing a lower volume of higher skill requirement than is available in the senior engineer ranks, there is a tendency to spread the work, filling in with lower grade activity, or even extending the time requirements for the higher grade work on a 'management judgement' basis. It may take some time to pick up the extent of under-employment in the senior ranks, possibly following the loss of some of the best people who have become dissatisfied with the lower level of demand placed on them. In this situation, you can be sure of one thing. The technical function will become deeply concerned about the losses, and the resulting shortage in the categories concerned. The manpower specialist needs to keep up his pressure on both the quality of standards, and the care monitoring of use of all technical manpower resources.

Marketing function

In the sales and marketing activities, we are concerned with the conversion of objectives and targets into the work to be done and how it is to be organised. Further, we must be especially ready to adapt to changes in strategy and objectives, and to tackle short-term 'discretionary-type' projects.

The proportionately large 'discretionary' or no-standards list needs to be kept under close control. Forecasts of future requirements must allow for yet-to-be-identified needs, probably following the pattern of the past, but varied for expectations of greater or lesser volumes of special activity.

The requirements for all activities where standards exist are reasonably straightforward, but it is difficult to assess the impact of a new product on the requirement for sales and marketing manpower, and probably advisable to leave a little slack in the forecasts. There is very rarely disadvantage in putting too much effort into marketing, but potentially serious disadvantage in under-resourcing this function.

A careful assessment of future competitor activity will be amongst the key assumptions used. Together with all assumptions, this needs to be kept under steady review, and forward manning projections modified as the assumptions are changed.

Personnel function

Numerically, this is a small function, perhaps half covered by manning standards and half by lists of no-standards and discretionary positions.

In a stable situation, new discretionary requirements tend to replace completed tasks and numbers stay reasonably constant. With a steady stream of new legislation affecting personnel, the need to review the company position on this alone generates a steady demand.

For areas with standards, we need to spot future activities which will impact on the work demand factor, or possibly make them obsolete. Changes in systems or in personnel policies may affect requirements in this way.

One additional factor could be a decision to increase the professionalism of the personnel function (equally applicable to other functions). Such a change of style invariably requires an increase in manpower for 1-2 years to support the launch of new activities and the re-education of management within the company.

Administration and finance

This is a reasonably straightforward area to cover, once the problems of defining necessary work have been resolved and the tendency to run to fat has been trimmed from the manning standards. The proportion of jobs without standards should be relatively low and easily controllable. The total picture should be capable of assembly for a series of points in time, with clear assumptions and without special difficulty.

Changing systems and equipment influence forward standards and needs more than is sometimes expected. Some of the changes we may expect over five years might include:

> More routine clerical functions will be superseded by computers, but the numbers of associated staff (programmers, operators, maintenance staff, and input/output data verifiers) will expand. Some copy and shorthand-typists will disappear and will be replaced by audio-typists operating from a central reservoir of office services. Micro-film units will store all correspondence, thus changing traditional filing activity. Looking further ahead, internal business mail, and perhaps ultimately external mail too, might one day pass directly, under computer control, from

a teleprinter in one office to the teleprinter in the office of the addressee.

There are other functions. I do not propose to cover these, for the principles are adequately illustrated by the categories discussed above.

One final point. Where does the supervisor or manager come into this picture? And how does he express his own view of manning requirements if these vary from 'official standards'. For me, something has gone wrong with the system if questions of this sort arise. It is important — it is essential — that supervisors and managers are so integrated into the system which establishes standards that the standards are theirs. They use them, trust them, try to improve them. If 'The Company' tries to change standards without involvement of these managers, it is creating a management aid unrelated to the realities of getting work done and will not effectively control the end result.

4.3   Requirement planning based on ratio-trends

Wherever the form of operations is at all static, or the pace of company evolution is slow, the existing manpower standards exert such a powerful influence on future standards that 'ratio-trend' provides a practical forecast.

The basic assumption being made is that the proportions of people to work required remain roughly the same, or that certain 'advantages of scale' will be evident so that growth or decline will approach a straight-line trend. In any event, past actual levels provide the 'manning standards' to be used to forecast future requirements.

Fundamentally, all manpower requirement forecasting is derived from analysis of the past. In 'ratio-trend' forecasting, we are accepting that the standards we should have as a base are not available, and we are using a cruder method likely to produce more generalised forecasts — but at least figures on which some further assumptions can be made. Alternatively, ratio-trend forecasts provide a cross-check on much more detailed forecasts developed from analyses of requirements by category, indicating whether the results of that detailed analysis conform to previous general patterns or whether some substantially different pattern is emerging.

Ratio-trend forecasting is based on the inertia that results from acceptance of existing manpower standards, and the problems of changing these standards. It accepts the relevance of applying existing standards to the planned work volumes to determine the future need, subject to no change in methods or standards taking place.

We may start off with an appraisal of the work requirements, and work out the precise manpower requirements on the basis of past ratios of work volume to number of staff:

1   Number of manual workers/number of units produced.
2   Number of salesmen/volume of orders.
3   Clerks/paper volume ratios.
4   Supervisor/staff ratios.

However, after approaching this simply, other factors can be seen to have come into play, such as:

1   The type of work, which may have varied somewhat since the original ratio was accepted.
2   The rate of output might be adjusted, or some other requirement.
3   The whole basis of activity may have changed, as it could in a situation of falling profitability.

Substantial changes also result from changes in the use of equipment, as in a factory which is gradually being automated, or an office where data-processing equipment is introduced.

To see this more clearly, and to form an impression of the range of factors which may be relevant in different circumstances, let us look at an actual case.

Company 'F' was expanding its field sales force very rapidly. It planned over the coming year to double the number of representatives and its number of sales managers. It had to consider what this would mean to its field sales administrative staff, as it was far from keen to double their numbers as well.

Two other factors influenced this situation; the first was that, with larger numbers of administrative staff, some increasing specialisation was possible with higher output per individual resulting. The second factor was that a clerical methods study was undertaken as part of the expansion programme and concentrated initially on the field operations. Streamlined administrative procedures were subsequently introduced and helped to cut growth of the administrative side to only one-third more people over the previous year.

Ratio-trend operation begins with the analysis of past staffing and the building up of ratio-trends to show what has happened to date. Basic manpower inventory provides a great deal of data for this operation. In addition to assembling data on meaningful relationships (we shall go into this further below), it is necessary to identify and record all those events which may be expected to link with a change in standards. Not all will be sudden changes, of course, as many developments are gradual, producing an effect over several months or years.

For this reason, apart from the advantages of using visual aids, it is almost essential to plot all this data on a series of ratio-trend graphs. These show clearly the sudden change in level or vector of some significant move, or equally well, the smooth curve of more gradual change. Figures 4.1 to 4.4 show ratio-trend graphs, some of which are explained in detail later in this chapter.

The key to effective ratio-trend operation appears to lie in the selection of meaningful ratios. By this, I mean that it is absolutely essential to link measurable amounts of work to manpower actively concerned in that work. Experience suggests that job analysis will indicate the bases to be used.

This analysis needs to be by job family groups, taken within the departments of the company, as work will also tend to be divisible by departments. For example, in a marketing department we might have:

1   Marketing manager.
2   A field sales manager and field sales supervisors (branch managers).
3   Salesmen.
4   Branch administrative staff.
5   A marketing planning manager.
6   Marketing planning officer, including market research, etc.
7   Administrative staff.

The manpower/work ratios might begin with salesmen/sales targets, salesmen/supervision, salesmen/branch administrative staff, and so on. The ratios selected must be meaningful in the situation, as the use of a relationship in which other factors have an influence

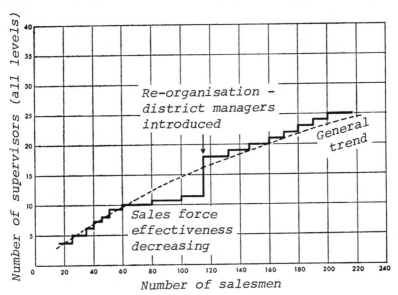

Figure 4.1 Ratio-trend graph: ratio of super-vision in field sales force

would result in the conclusions being misleading if applied.

Line and staff activities respond rather differently to this type of analysis. Line activities, with their direct productive nature, are ideally suited, so that production and sales departments present few difficulties. Relationships between work required and manpower directly employed are straightforward, and similar ratios of close supporting staff are also relevant.

In 'staff' areas, work is less easily measured in any standard and continuing unit form. Staff 'service' activities fall between the two categories. For example, the finance department's billing section produces a measurable number of units, and even the personnel department's recruitment officer has a measurable output! But not so the research department. Its team of electronics engineers may have quadrupled over the past two years, and they may have produced some valuable results, but the results are 'one-off' and future objectives are not assessable in the same terms. Only an assessment of engineers required to achieve the work planned can determine whether seven or fourteen or twenty-one engineers will be needed next year. Or the question could well be reversed to ask: 'What can be achieved with the engineers we can obtain?'

Ratios for staff departments cannot generally be developed with any continuing standards, and the relationship between their costs and total company income, or between their manpower and company total manpower, or some other ratio which is related to the company's environment, represents the limit one can go to with this

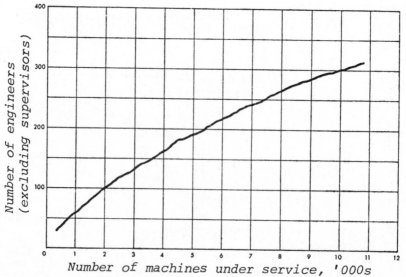

Figure 4.2 Ratio-trend graph: ratio of service engineers to machines in field

group by the ratio-trend method. It is more relevant to consider company objectives and the expectations from staff departments as a basis for determining staff needs.

Returning to line operations, look at some figures for an office-equipment company with a substantial service force. In this rather straightforward case, there is a direct relationship between numbers of machines potentially requiring service, and numbers of engineers. Variation occurs in areas where machines are fewer and more scattered, requiring greater travelling and non-working time than where the machines are concentrated into a small area. Future variation may occur if different types of machine, with different service requirements, must be covered.

Figure 4.2 shows a trend line drawn through the total number of machines/total number of engineers. Figure 4.3 on double log-

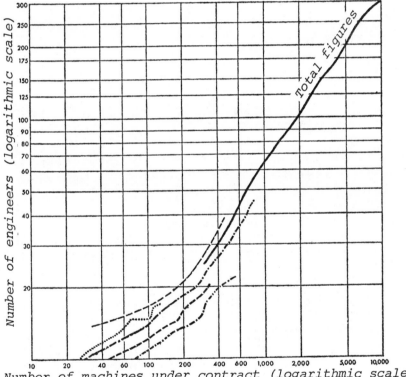

Figure 4.3 Ratio-trend graph: ratio of service engineers to machines in field, by district. (Note: variations of ratios are partially due to length of time the district has been established, i.e. number of older machines, and partly due to the spread of territory and density of machines

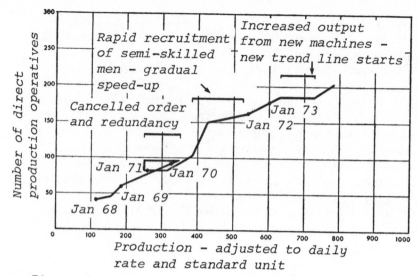

Figure 4.4 Ratio-trend graph: ratio of operatives to production

paper, brings out the variation that occurs between small and large areas.

Almost any activity can be examined in this way, and relationships drawn out between manpower categories and measures of the work they do.

Keeping things straightforward for a moment and following on from the service engineer example above, associated relationships were found in that company between:

1   Salesmen and machines sold
2   Direct production employees and production
3   Administrative support staff and the employee group supported (separate relationships for service, sales, production)
4   Overseas activities and home-based divisions
and finally,
5   Overall manpower and total business (measured in financial or other terms).

It was possible to note significant developments and resultant changes in trend lines on the charts, and in extending trend lines, to take anticipated developments into account. In this way, optimum manning of all new situations became a possibility which could be blended into the existing pattern.

1   Specifically, a new product to sell, and changing market conditions requiring new objectives, are likely to alter the trend lines. But as a short-term measure, why not relate the new situation back to the old?
2   How much time should the new machine take to sell in

relation to the old, and to its relative profitability?

3   How much time needs to be allocated to the new require-
     ments of the market? (More 'public relations' calls on
     established customers to offset an opposition advertising
     campaign, perhaps.)
4   How much time on changed administrative methods? How
     much time on regular training sessions?
5   If changes are being properly planned, it must be possible to
     appraise the expected effect, for few managements change
     course without assessing what will happen.

In some of the examples quoted, there is a high correlation
between total manpower required and one particular 'work demand
factor', to the point where it is possible to read a requirement
figure off a graph against any planned volume. From this type of
data, it is also possible to define the relationship between the
variables in a simple formula:

$$y = a + bx$$

where y is the manpower requirement, x the 'work demand factor'
and a and b are constants. If the formula is applied to a manufacturing situation, then a will evidently define the fixed manpower level
associated with support services which changes to a minimal degree
with volume change, while b is a factor connecting the units of work
in the work demand factor to the variable manning requirement
associated directly with volume change. Of course, a and b are not
precisely as indicated as there will be an additional variable
incorporated associated with higher productivity on higher volumes.
As an example, the formula might produce:

$$y \text{ (manpower requirement)} = 45 + 12 \times 14 \text{ 'units'}$$
$$= 45 + 168$$
$$= 213 \text{ men}$$

or for a smaller volume
$$y = 45 + 12 \times 7$$
$$= 45 + 84$$
$$= 129 \text{ men}$$

Such a formula will have been developed from part operational data,
and provided the production volume required does not go outside
that experience, should prove reasonably accurate. However, if
volume is to be stepped up to a level 30 per cent above previous
experience, the formula can provide no more than a starting point
number which must be proven by other means — for example, by
confirming that the organisation structure can remain unchanged,

　and that no new equipment or skills will be brought in, etc.

Of course, manpower is rarely dependant on one variable. It may be that you would like to proceed into more complex mathematics, and this is certainly possible, but from practical experience of the accuracy possible in real life situations, I believe that a single variable (or at the most two variables), provided we take time to identify them properly, give the optimum working result. My personal choice then is to place emphasis on identifying meaningful work demand factors rather than engage in pseudo-scientific formulae which give an appearance of science, but poor forecasts.

Probably, ratio-trend is most suited to production line-type situations, and other manpower-intensive areas with relatively standard work type. New production lines can be planned for, with planned output and manning levels based very simply on previous standards.

Other manpower ratios

There are many simple ratios which are used from time to time on manpower comparisons, which influence managements to accept or reject manpower forecasts. The simplest of all are produced from comparison of any work factor with the manning used as proposed. Movements in the ratio will tend to show changing productivity, or the intervention of some other factor.

For example, the level of sales compared with number of salesmen may be as shown in Table 4.2. After making allowances for inflation in excess of 10 per cent a year, these figures are certainly

TABLE 4.2

	Sales, £000s	Number of salesmen	Average sales, £000s
Year 1 actual	100	10	10
Year 2 actual	120	12	10
Year 3 actual	180	15	12
Year 4 forecast	240	18	13

not spectacular, using average sales per salesman as the key ratio. Most companies would seek a better performance than that shown.

A second ratio which is widely used is comparison of total remuneration with total sales or with added value. Neither is an ideal comparison, as the ratio with sales may be blurred by changing

volumes of sub-contract work or resale of manufactured goods,
while added value needs precise definition, and is less clearly understood.

Even so, year-to-year changes in these key ratios deserve very
careful analysis so that the reasons for change are fully understood.
A steadily rising remuneration to sales ratio should highlight the
probability of steady build up of non-essential manpower which is
almost certainly eroding the company's profit margins.

4.4 Contingency planning

In the preparation of a business plan, a number of possible
occurrences will be identified that are considered to be unlikely —
but which may develop. Where the probability of such an event
is sufficiently high for it to be taken seriously, a contingency plan
should be developed setting out the actions that will be taken in
response.

The most common types of events covered by contingency
plans include greater or lesser volumes of orders, and therefore
manufacture; earlier or delayed timing of technical change; timing
or impact of legislation (or even change of government).

We are concerned here with the impact on manpower requirement
planning and the mechanisms that we can plan and use in the event
of short-term change of plan. The actions will vary depending on the
nature of the change, whether it involves increased or decreased
activity and whether the change is expected to be of short duration
or become more or less permanent. The various options from which
actions can be selected are examined individually.

Sub-contract work   An unexpected order which cannot be met by
existing resources may be partially sub-contracted, particularly
where the higher volume required is not expected to be permanent.
If order volume falls away but management wishes to retain the work
force against future demand, it is possible sometimes, to obtain
additional short-term work of a sub-contract nature, usually at low
margins but adequate to cover overheads.

Overtime or short-time working   Within the current work force
there is usually the capacity for a $\pm$ 20 per cent variation of working
hours from use of heavy overtime or of brief periods of short-time
working. Employee acceptance of these arrangements will be understood by the company so that the extent they can be built into plans
will be pre-determined.

Additional shifts It is sometimes possible to introduce an evening shift where equipment is limited and greater utilisation is required. Such arrangements take some time to build up and are not lightly discarded, but may serve to meet a peak workload of 1-2 years.

Temporary employees   If the nature of a peak load is somewhat different from the normal run of work, it may be logical to introduce the additional skills required in the form of temporary employees, either from a contract staff agency, or on a fixed-period contract. However, these are not always acceptable practices and permanent employees may raise objections, usually related to the special terms and conditions of the temporary staff.

Reduction techniques   If it should become necessary to reduce manning levels suddenly, some advance preparation against the possibility can be made. For example, retention of a high proportion of employees for up to five years over normal retirement age both limits the need to recruit people who could become redundant at an early stage, and provides a means for a sharp reduction by returning to normal retirement practice. Further, opportunities for advantageous early retirement for those within five years of retirement dates provide acceptable scope for further easy reduction.

Immediate total restructuring of recruitment is an obvious course of action, while normal wastage rates among shorter-service employees will also help to reduce the total manpower.

If the restructuring requirement is so substantial that redundancy is unavoidable, a great deal depends on the extent of the 'early warning' and the generosity of redundancy terms. Many companies achieve redundancies without industrial action, and even manage to expedite the process by offering 'quick release' bonuses. However, it is preferable to spread the release times and do everything possible to assist employees to find other jobs, to the extent of extensive counselling and the setting up of 'job shops' on the premises where other employers may be offered interview facilities.

Planning to provide short-term flexibility of manpower is an important subsidiary area for manpower requirement planning — and an area where substantial success is possible.

4.5   Manpower requirement summary

Analyses of the types described above produce a comprehensive picture of the posts expected to exist. To see this picture clearly requires detailed analysis which builds up as a summary showing how many jobs of each type will exist. These analyses will provide the lead into the next phase of manpower supply planning, covered in Chapter 7. For this reason, I will be repeating some of the examples used here in the later chapter, and will concentrate here on requirement summaries.

Seeking out practical examples I found these comparatively rare in the 'pure requirements' form. Almost invariably, the act of summarising requirements was followed with an immediate rough assessment of how the requirements were to be met.

Table 4.1, used at the beginning of the chapter, is something of a rarity for this reason. It shows only the planned forward requirements, in summary form over a two-year period, concentrating on the timing of the requirements. As previously noted, there would be supporting analyses on sourcing to ensure provision of manpower to schedule.

Table 4.3 shows a summary sheet (which includes some additional data on supply). The fineness of the breakdown is discretionary, subject to it being meaningful in the particular case. In the example used, the separate identification of management positions shows detail of the timing of requirements which could equally well have been covered by footnotes. This stage is particularly vital as it is the basis for comparison with the internal manpower supply, and leads on to calculations of anticipated external manpower requirements.

Once the summary of future posts has been completed and analysed, the probable development of existing staff can be better assessed against the background of possible vacancies. From this appraisal, a complete summary of future vacancies which cannot be filled by existing staff can be seen. This summary, with the final addition of replacement for losses, gives the calculated requirement of manpower during the period. These further stages are detailed in Chapter 7.

Table 4.4 shows a group summary which is more generalised in nature. At the beginning of the summary, the current positions in a series of subsidiaries are shown, together with totals, followed by data on the total extent of change expected over a five-year period. This presentation is invaluable for giving an overall view of the scale of problems, for discussion at board level, but it can be rather misleading about timing.

Summaries of manpower requirements, and appropriate costings, are essential inputs to business planning. The costing is usually more significant at this stage than expected headcount, although questions of housing and equipping increasing numbers of people need to be identified and fully covered in the plan.

Table 4.5 shows a business plan summary covering the next two years, illustrating the changes expected by major functions and divided into direct and indirect categories. Cost figures are added below. It is, of course, possible to 'explode' this data into something far more complex if you wish, for the background detail should

Table 4.3 Manpower requirement forecasts (extract from working sheet)

Job category	Strength at 1.1.1976	1977				1978				End 1979	End 1980	End 1981	Notes
		End 1st qtr.	End 2nd qtr.	End 3rd qtr.	End 4th qtr.	End 1st qtr.	End 2nd qtr.	End 3rd qtr.	End 4th qtr.				
Applications engineering department:													
Manager	1	1	1	1	1	1	1	1	1	1	1	1	
Head – customer service	1	1	1	1	1	1	1	1	1	3	3	3	Regional breakdown 1979
Head – application research	–	–	1	1	1	1	1	1	1	1	1	1	Vacancy advertised
Head – applications library	–	–	–	–	–	–	1	1	1	1	1	1	Part of regionalisation plan
Senior engineer	7	7	8	8	9	9	9	10	10	15	15	15	F/C on work analysis
Applications engineer (a)	18	19	20	21	22	23	24	25	26	30	34	38	(a) Ratio-trend F/C (not used)
(b)	18	18	20	20	22	24	26	29	34	35	42	50	(b) F/C on work analysed
Research engineer	–	–	–	2	2	2	3	3	3	4	5	6	
Technical assistant (a)	20	21	22	23	24	25	26	27	28	32	36	40	(a) Ratio-trend (not used)
(b)	20	20	20	18	18	18	18	20	20	22	24	26	(b) Work analysed F/C used

Forecast strengths – 5-year forecast

Etc.

Table 4.4 Building group manpower requirements areas

Category	End 1977 actuals				1977 Total	End 1982 forecast total		Estimated loss rates inc retirement		Estimated promotions required		Estimated requirement from outside group	
	Company A	B	C	D		Inc	Total	%	Total over 5 years	Promotion from	Promotion to	Total over 5 years	Aver. annual rate
MD/Manager	1	1	2	1	5	−1	4	—	1	—	—	—	—
Branch Manager	—	—	1	—	1	−3	4	—	1	—	2	2	—
Chief Contr Mgr/Dir	1	1	—	—	2	—	2	—	—	—	—	—	—
Contract Managers	8	5	3	3	19	+3	22	10%	10	1	3	11	2
Foremen	13	12	20	—	45	+10	55	20%	50	3	20	43	9
Trainee/Asst Foremen	11	7	3	3	24	+41	65	20%	44	20	—	105	21
Chief Surveyor	1	1	2	—	4	—	4	10%	2	—	2	—	—
Surveyors	10	8	3	1	22	3	25	15%	18	2	12	11	2
Asst/Trainees	—	—	1	—	1	11	12	20%	6	12	—	29	6
Chief Est/Plnrs/Buyer	2	2	2	—	6	2	8	10%	3	—	2	3	1
Est/Plnrs/Buyers	—	4	4	2	10	4	14	15%	9	2	4	9	2
Asst/Trainee Est/Plr/Buyer	1	—	—	—	1	11	12	20%	6	4	—	21	4

TABLE 4.5 Business plan summary of manpower requirements and remuneration

Manpower category	Planned year end 1977	Change 1978	Planned year end 1978	Change	Planned year end 1979
DIRECT:					
Manufacturing	2074	143	2217	191	2408
Engineering	245	35	280	20	300
Distribution	301	(12)	289	3	292
Total:	2620	166	2786	214	3000
INDIRECT:					
Manufacturing	305	4	309	10	319
Engineering	48	1	49	6	55
Distribution	35	(3)	32	(2)	30
Marketing	86	(6)	80	8	88
Admin & Finance	134	14	148	–	148
Total:	608	10	618	22	640
GRAND TOTAL	3228	176	3404	236	3640
REMUNERATION	£12.27m	£1.22m	£13.49m	£2.01m	£15.50m

Table 4.6 Departmental one-year manpower requirement forecast

Types of jobs	Number of staff at	Anticipated loss		Anticipated gain transfer/promotion	Net	Total requirement forecast at	Balance required during forecast year
		Terminations	Transfer/promotion				
Department manager	1				1	1	—
Cost accountant	1				1	1	—
Billing supervisor	1				1	1	—
Accounting operations supervisor	1		1*	1	1	1	—
Assistant accountant	1			1	2	2	—
Cashier	1		1		1	1	—
Book-keeper	2				1	2	+1
Accounting operations clerk	6	2	1	1	4	6	+2
Billing clerk	5	1			4	5	+1
Records clerk	2	1			1	2	+1
Filing clerk	1				1	1	—
Secretary	1				1	1	—
Shorthand typist	2	1			1	2	+1
Billing typist	5	2			3	5	+2

* To H.Q. Dept.

exist. Further, the manpower numbers used are year-end figures, where some other organisations prefer to use average numbers (which tie in better with total remuneration).

For more complete detail on requirement plan summaries and the further stage of supply planning, please see Section 7.1.

Special cases

Before leaving requirement planning completely, I would like to comment on some of the unusual situations which occur, for which special treatment is necessary.

Growth companies   In fast-growing companies, the number of jobs at, say, director level may not change significantly, but the grading or value denoting the size of responsibility and complexity of these jobs may increase rapidly. In growth situations, the number of employees may double or treble at lower levels of clerical and manual workers and their supervisors. Growth means only more jobs at the same levels. At the top of the company, job values may gradually double as responsibilities grow rapidly.

Between the static job values at the base of the pyramid and the rising peak of the growing structure additional levels are created, with some jobs growing and rising, and others remaining more static and being 'capped' by additional supervisory levels. It is important that these phenomena of job growth in a growing organisation are recognised in organisation, manpower and career planning. The post of marketing director existing in a company for ten or 20 years will change over the years. The change may result in a series of developments and the type of man needed to do the job may change – perhaps several times. Where this change is very fast, the altering requirement must be acknowledged in the manpower plan, so that the job is identified as a series of separate posts with distinct specifications.

Where possible – in other words wherever a grading structure exists – forecasts of grade levels should be developed in parallel with job requirement records, and the requirements against each grade level analysed. While this does not tell the whole story, such an analysis can be extremely informative. Table 4.6 shows a forecast of such a situation which adds significantly to an appreciation of the problems.

The young division   Most companies set up a new division, a new department, or some form of new organisation from time to time. Up to a point, these new organisations can be planned for and staff developed in advance to fill the key posts. But, more often than not, the planning does not begin sufficiently in advance for the team to be prepared to the ordered specification. Here, the aim is one of preparing sufficient people to man possible new divisions, if and when the company engages in defined new activities.

One of the major companies in the paper industry adopted the deliberate policy of overstaffing with high-potential people to meet the requirements of new departments or product divisions. The result was a useful stock of experienced people, but a higher than usual turnover of those good people. The company accepted this situation and was able, from time to time, to meet a sudden demand for additional managers following some commercial development. However, the approach was costly and caused as many problems as it solved.

Other companies have found it necessary to recruit whole teams externally to meet the management requirements of a new organisation.

A detailed inventory of existing skills, experience and potential provides the best defence when a new unit is proposed at short notice. Existing strength can then be displayed to optimum advantage to cover the immediate situation.

Ideally, we should think immediately of the potential staffing problems whenever a new organisation of any sort is considered. Then, as it 'jells', the staffing plan can gradually consolidate and machinery to build up a probable team can be quietly running, well before the final decisions to go ahead are taken. If the planning and staff development moves are unobtrusive, any revision of the organisation plan need not be disastrous, and management potential will have been built up which may be applied elsewhere if the planned new division is abandoned.

Fast evolution   The discovery of a new process raises similar problems, except that the time from notice to action will normally be shorter. A small company is invariably forced to look outside at such a time, while a larger organisation may be able to redeploy resources internally. From a long-term planning point of view, one cannot anticipate the unforeseeable. Not once in a hundred times will a research team be able to indicate, years ahead, the date of availability, form, practicability and marketability of a new idea — and, even then, no one will believe them!

In the central staff of Company H, a production advisory service was created. The function of this small organisation was to assist in solving major production problems in all divisions of the company.

With time, the demands for this service grew steadily and, as it became understood, the type of query posed became more complex and more difficult to solve, the smaller problems being handled on site by local production engineers.

The forward manpower plan for this central team involved no build-up in numbers of staff, but increasing specialisation, technological change, and a substantial raising of influence and of job values over a period of time. This involved the transfer of no-longer-required people from the centre and re-staffing with individuals of outstanding ability and relevant know-how. While numbers and job titles remained unchanged, development required the transfer of 60 per cent of the team each two-year period.

The entrepreneur In a large private company I know of, the top man announced a new venture — to be put into operation immediately. As the new venture was to have a seven-figure turnover within a year, a great deal of furious 'pirating' was essential to obtain the necessary staff. In spite of the skills which were pressed into operation, there must have been a substantial element of luck in the successful, but scrambled, launch of this new enterprise.

It was put to me that the entrepreneurial attitude and planning do not mix. True enough, I suppose, but they do need to coexist peacefully so that the ground is prepared in advance for major developments in the way outlined for the 'young division' above.

Not all ideas come to fruition, so why plan? The answer, I think, is that the planning study is likely to confirm or refute the soundness of the proposal and so encourage either its speedy and successful launch or its logical cancellation.

MANPOWER INFORMATION SYSTEM

A complete study of your manpower information system will probably surprise you, in terms of the considerable volume of diverse data absorbed into the system, and the volume of output. You may also be surprised by the volume of data absorbed but never used and, depending on your system, the extreme difficulty of converting raw data to useful information.

I shall assume that your organisation employs a thousand or more people, and that you have developed computerised systems to handle your manpower data. If you have yet to computerise, it is essential to develop your system carefully and ensure quality of output, as to impose a system on existing chaos can do no more than make the chaos formal — and much more difficult to change.

It is also worth remembering that a systems specialist will only design a system to stated requirements; if you do not specify your needs properly, you may never obtain your full requirements. This chapter is structured to look first at the required *outputs* from a manpower information system, and then at the various *inputs* necessary. It does not go into detail on the technical aspects of systems or investigate the logic of blending the manpower system with payroll requirements.

In the climate of stability or growth, when manpower shortages may impose restrictions on achieving business objectives, the case for improving the efficiency of personnel administration systems is easily made. In a climate of changing technology, changing manpower requirements impose a great strain on a computerised personnel record system. Changing manpower requirements may lead to:

1   Imbalances in age/grade/length of service profiles.

2   Gaps in key functions/appointments.
3   Shortage of high-calibre employees.
4   Limited career opportunities.
5   Promotion blockages.
6   Embarrassing surpluses in non-key areas.
7   Decaying salary structures.
8   'Slippage' in job description and accountability.
The information system must provide adequate diagnosis of these problems or we are not in a position to take effective action.

Changing technology occurs in both changing methods of production and in the product itself. Product life-cycles have become shorter, imposing a need for faster response to problems and perhaps a more flexible approach. We are faced with the considerable restructuring of the human resource in:

a   Numbers — we shall need far fewer people for many activities.
b   Skills — early indications of impact on skill requirements shows considerable de-skilling of many jobs.
c   Changing work patterns — from group or team activities to one-man operations.
d   Many direct operations will be phased out and past indirect/direct ratios are not relevant.
e   New jobs may become 'key' jobs requiring new methods of resourcing.
f   If we become more capital intensive we become more manpower sensitive.
g   Lead times for high technological skills will be longer and therefore training and development schemes more critical.

The magnitude and relative importance of these problems cannot be determined without reference to quantitative techniques.

As we develop our manpower there is need to improve the utilisation of this resource. If we become more automated we will need to concentrate on the manning of fewer but key positions.

There is increasing need to justify personnel policy to external bodies; in planning agreements; in race relations and sex discrimination legislation; etc. Further, there is a requirement to give prior notification of some activities to executive branches of the Manpower Services Commission — DoE, ESA, TSA. There is a continuing need to provide the trade unions with selected information. These information requirements will increase.

Our objectives should be to:

1   Provide management information in a manageable form that would otherwise by unobtainable due to the cost and/or manual effort involved.
2   Provide data which is appropriate, comprehensive and timely and focuses attention on areas where management effort will be best rewarded.

3   Prepare all routine reports/listings/forms for internal and
     external use thereby reducing non-productive manual tasks,
     thus freeing staff for work where their expertise can be fully
     utilised.
4   Determine methods of simplifying data capture and record
     maintenance to minimise effort at input points.

It would be wrong to assume that all computerised systems are
free of fault. The most common failures are associated with any
one or a combination of the following:

a   The 'all-singing, all-dancing' system designed to produce
     innumerable complex outputs and consequently requiring a
     heavy input, usually resulting in high workload for little result.
b   Lack of understanding or fear of computers lead many users
     to abdicate from their decision-making responsibilities. This
     often leads to fundamental misunderstandings in systems
     design and concept.
c   Setting unreal targets and unrealistically high expectations
     which lead only to disappointments and sometimes the
     termination of the project as a whole.
d   Insufficient understanding of the additional complexity
     introduced into systems thinking by processing information
     relating to people. Mistakes which might be thought minor in
     other systems are highly visible and highly subjective. People
     are dynamic elements in any system.

The above points only become apparent after the system is in full
operation when it is difficult, somtimes impossible, and always
costly to amend.

The major burden of file maintenance falls on line personnel
departments. Since the value of the system depends on the validity
of its input, line personnel have a very important role to play.

A computer can deal easily with diverse and complex problems,
but when designing a system it is unlikely that every future
requirement will be foreseen. If the system is sub-divided into a
series of 'stand alone' functional modules drawing data from a
master file, new requirements may be more easily met. Some
suggested modules might be:

Basic Personnel Record
Personnel Analyses
Salary Administration
Training and Development
Industrial Relations
Manpower Planning
Manpower Costs
Social Justification

The exact format and structure of the modules will be up to the
user.

A modular method has these advantages:

1   There is a perceivable return on outlay at an early stage. As each module is completed, outputs are produced, thus minimising the long delay between the workload of data capture and the use of results.
2   Learning can be built up over a period of time and mistakes can be corrected before they pollute the entire system.
3   The development can be controlled, directing effort to modules as required by the user. (It is assumed priorities will be determined on a cost-effective basis.)
4   Should the development be called to a halt there is a valid and operable system in use. The system is capable of development and further evolution at a later stage.

5.1   Required outputs

The whole purpose of the manpower information system is to get the outputs required, at the right time, in the right format, and integrated with other numbers coming from other parts of the company information systems. It is essential that the manpower system is fully integrated with the overall company systems and in no way isolated or separate.

The most obvious point of wider contact is payroll, and many manpower information systems have built up from the payroll — frequently one of the first company activities to be transferred to the computer.

I propose to set out many of the outputs generally required from a comprehensive system, with brief notes. While this may be used as a checklist, it is likely that individual requirements will add to and delete from this list.

Salary review

Salary listing for salary review purposes.

Salary review analyses and summaries.

Salary drift/wage drift, by grades, plants, etc.

Compa-ratios; movements in average salaries by grade.

Performance rating analyses.

Grading: distribution by grade within departments, divisions, etc.

Salary distribution: salary scatter within grade salary ranges, by occupation group, or area, or division, etc.

Record sheet reproductions from central file.

Control listing for short lists, etc., against all vacancies before external action.

Nominal roll by division, department, cost centre for audit against budget, etc.

Training release: part-time day release statistics, sandwich students, etc.

Leavers: analysis of numbers, reasons for leaving, categories leaving, etc.

Retirements: current and future.

Long-service awards: current and future.

Returns to DoE, EITB, EEF: routine production of required statistics.

Manpower utilisation

Occupation analysis: including analysis of levels.

Age distribution: against grade, salary, by department, etc.

Skill utilisation; skills and qualifications in relation to occupation type and level.

Headcount control: in relation to budget or establishment, suitably flexed for changes in work volume.

Promotion analysis: 'throughput' rates of people by category and grade level.

Grade analysis: against many factors: salary, age, by division, etc.

Mobility analysis; potential ability to transfer to other areas or occupations including thorough retraining and redeployment to related skill areas.

Industrial relations and social justification

Race relations: distribution of coloured and other workers by pay and status, length of service, etc.

Equal opportunity: as race relations.

Planning agreements: manpower requirement plans arising from planning agreements.

Wage distribution: in relation to service, merit, etc.

Union membership: for representation queries, for deduction of union dues.

Union training time.

Pensions, medical

Sickness absence: by cause, department, occupation, etc., and by frequency for individuals.

Absence reports.

Health and safety statistics.

Disability ratios.

DoE pensions.

5.2 Required inputs (personnel records, etc.)

All the data mentioned so far, and a great deal more which is known about employees, will be stored in some sort of personnel records system. Apart from an 'everything' type dossier, all current and significant data is likely to be contained in a straightforward card system as illustrated in Figure 5.1. This shows a record card style which I have found useful personally, one which was matched with magnetic type records for analyses using EDP. However, there are very many variants and you must find a format which gives your organisation the data it needs in readily visible form.

Assembly of accurate basic data and careful maintenance subsequently are both of major importance if we are to avoid 'rubbish in − rubbish out' in our analyses. A clear system for updating at regular and frequent intervals, fully appreciated by all users, seems to be the key.

One set of personnel data that is kept very much up to date is the payroll. To the extent that personnel records and payroll can be closely linked, we can be sure that a lump of the most critical data will indeed be properly maintained. This will include name (which can change, of course), job data, job grade, salary data, pension and other benefit membership, bonus and overtime earnings, and a few other items. With the concept of a total, integrated management information system becoming more usual, the incentive to link

personnel records and payroll is strong. For the personnel manager,
his major benefit may be the end of differences between his records
and the number of people actually paid.

What we shall call the 'data elements' required within the total
manpower information systems are covered in the section which
follows:

1   Identification:
Surname and forenames.
Maiden name.
Works or computer reference number specific to the individual.

2   Other personal information:
Address (including postal code) and telephone number.
Next of kin.
Date of birth.
Sex.
Marital state.
Alien (if relevant) and work permit detail.
Immigrant/colour — for analysis of race relations practice.
Registered disabled person — if relevant.
Trade union membership.
Relatives with company.

3   Organisation/location:
Company or division within group.
Location.
Department.
Cost centre reference number.

4   Occupation history:
(a)   Prior to joining company:
—   Employers.
—   Position held.
—   Dates.
(b)   Date of joining:
Details of 'broken service' — if relevant.
Recruiting source.
Status of employment: full time, part time, temporary or contract.
Positions held within company:
—   Dates appointed.
—   Job titles and departments.
—   Job grades.
—   Occupation codes.

Employee's no.	Surname		Mr/Mrs Miss	First names		
Date of Birth — Day / Month / Year	Marital status	Code	Maiden name if married woman	Nationality	Code	PHOTOGRAPH HERE
Naturalization no. or alien's registration no.		R.D.P. no.		Nationality at birth if different		
Home address	Telephone no.	Photograph data: Date taken: Negative no:				
		Next of kin (name, address and relationship). Tel. no.				

Dates From / To	Secondary schools, universities, technical colleges	Examinations – subjects, results and dates	Code

Professional qualifications and societies	By election	By exam.	Grade of membership	Year	Code

Dates From / To	Previous employment including forces service (most recent first)			
	Name, location & business of employers	Brief description of jobs held	Reason for leaving	

Foreign languages				Code	Training courses attended (internal and external)	Dates	Code
Language	R	S	W	Comments on fluency			

Previous rank organization service	Dates	Code		

Apprenticeship: firm		Code	Tests	Code
Type	Dates: 19 to 19			

Date of and reason for leaving	Reason code — 1st / 2nd	Re-engage Yes/No		

Figure 5.1a Staff records card

5 Salaries and benefits:

Salary history:
- Basic salary or wages.
- Bonus, supplementary payments, etc.
- Dates and amounts of changes.
- Reasons for changes.
- Planned next change: amount and date.

Hours:
- Normal hours.
- Overtime paid/not paid.
- Shiftwork.

Employee's no.	Surname		Initials	Sex	Date of birth			Date of engagement			Adjusted date of engagement		
				M F	Day	Month	Year	Day	Month	Year	Day	Month	Year

Date joined pension scheme	National insurance no.	Basic weekly hours		

JOB DETAILS

Date	Cost centre code	Division	Department	Job title	Job no.	Job grade	Reason for job change

REMUNERATION DETAILS

Date	Job grade	Appraisal		Last adjustment to basic salary		Bonus/ Commission		Gross annual pensionable pay	Allowances	
		Perform	Potential	Amount	Code	Amount	Code		Amount	Code

Figure 5.1b Staff records card

Benefits eligibility/awarded:
— Holiday entitlement.
— Company car.
— BUPA.
— Company loan, etc.

Pension scheme membership:
— Scheme.
— Date joined.
— Normal retirement date.
— Life assurance cover, etc.

6   *Performance and potential assessment:*
Most recent performance data.
Most recent data covering potential.
Psychological test score, results and dates.
Planned next position (if relevant):
—   Position.
—   Occupation code.
—   Job grade.
—   Timing.

7   *Qualifications:*
—   Level ('O' level/'A' level/degree/doctorate).
—   Field.
—   Specialist/professional.
—   Apprenticeship, etc.

8   *Training received:*
Training courses attended:
—   Internal/external.
—   Level of course.
—   Duration.
—   Dates.
Training planned.

9   *Skills:*
Skills outside current sphere of activity.
Languages, etc.

10   *Medical history (confidential — restricted access).*

11   *Absenteeism.*

12   *Overtime/shift-work/part-time work.*

Much of this information will need coding to facilitate inclusion in the computerised system and to simplify analysis. It is relatively easy to code such things as location, division, department and cost centre, and these are probably well covered by established codes for wider purposes within the company. Similarly, academic qualifications or reasons for leaving are easily coded; experience in other fields is more difficult to code.

The most important coding task is occupation coding. Some ten years ago, I was involved in creating from scratch a coding based on job families and built up in decimalised form to provide full detail We made some use of the ILO Standard Classification of Occupations.

Today, the Department of Employment system known as CODOT (Classification of Occupation and Directory of Occupational Titles) provides an excellent base, on to which finer detail required within the company may be grafted. (The alternative, IMSSOC, of the Institute of Manpower Studies, I personally find difficult to use in industry.)

CODOT provides a classification system to cover all occupations found in Great Britain, although distinctions between occupations are generally made only when they are considered to be of value for employment or statistical purposes. This results in about 3500 separately identified occupations, each of which is adequately defined.

Occupations are identified and grouped primarily in terms of the work usually performed, this being determined by the tasks, duties and responsibilities of the occupation. Occupations are not identified and grouped primarily in terms of the industry in which the worker is employed nor by his level of authority, skill or qualifications, because these are regarded as additional facets of occupations. However, these facets are implicit in some CODOT occupational groupings, for example:

1   Occupations specific to an individual industry are grouped together.
2   Levels of authority between worker and supervisor, between supervisor and manager and between manager and general manager are recognised because they are reflected in the nature of the work performed.
3   Grouping by work performed inevitably brings together many occupations of similar skill levels.
4   Qualifications are usually mentioned when they have some legal significance, e.g. in medicine and law, but in general the performance of tasks and duties takes precedence over possession of formal qualifications.

The principle of identifying and grouping occupations according to work performed is followed in two other standard works, the International Standard Classification of Occupations (ISCO) and the classification used by the Office of Population Censuses and Surveys for analysis of census data. The three classifications have considerable compatibility.

The 3500 occupations are grouped at three levels to show wider occupational relationships and to identify groups of general significance for manpower planning. These levels are:

Unit group   a basic group of occupations in which the main tasks are similar. The occupations in a unit group are related to each other more in terms of work performed than to occupations outside the group.

Minor group   a collection of unit groups related in terms of work performed.

Major group   a convenient collection of minor groups to assist in comprehension of the classification as a whole.

There are 378 unit groups, 73 minor groups and 18 major groups. The 3500 occupations are therefore structured in a four-tier system of classification which can be operated at different levels of refinement to suit the varying needs of users. *Gaps are left throughout the code numbering system so that finer distinctions between occupations can be introduced to suit particular needs of users.*

Following the title of each major and minor group there is a brief general definition of the type of work included in the group and a list of the code numbers and titles of its component minor and unit groups, respectively (see Figure 5.2). Following each unit group title is a more detailed description of the work covered by the occupations in the group.

Occupational definitions come after unit group definitions and include five basic components:

1   Flag statements   a short opening statement giving the essential characteristics of the occupation in terms of the work performed.

2   'How' items   a series of short statements describing the main tasks normally carried out in the occupation. On occasions, these are replaced by a cross-reference to a base definition or to the definition of a closely related occupation, thereby avoiding repetition of the main tasks common to a number of occupations.

3   'May' items   when appropriate, a few short statements, indicating common specialisations within the occupation and tasks additional to those implicit in the flag statement which are often associated with the occupation.

4   Additional factors   as necessary, a statement of factors that are important when considering employment in the occupation.

5   Other titles   which are used for various jobs covered by the

225 Chemical Engineering Research and Development, Design, Feasibility Studies, Applications, Liaison, Consultancy and Related Occupations

225.00 Manager
225.11 General chemical engineer (general chemical engineering)
225.12 General chemical engineer (heavy chemicals)
225.13 General chemical engineer (fine chemicals)
225.14 General chemical engineer (synthetic resins and plastics)
225.15 General chemical engineer (petroleum)
225.19 General chemical engineer (other chemical engineering)
225.21 Chemical engineer (research and development) (general chemical engineering)
225.22 Chemical engineer (research and development) (heavy chemicals)
225.23 Chemical engineer (research and development) (fine chemicals)

860 Foremen (Construction and Related Occupations Not Elsewhere Classified)

860.05 Foreman bricklayer
860.10 Foreman fixer mason
860.15 Foreman plasterer
860.20 Foreman (terrazzo working, tile setting occupations)
860.25 Foreman (roofing occupations)
860.30 Foreman glazier
860.35 Foreman (road making and repairing occupations) (excluding machine operating)
860.40 Foreman (trackmen and platelayers)
860.45 Area works inspector (railway)
860.50 Permanent way inspector (railway)
860.55 Foreman (concrete erecting occupations)
860.98 Trainee
860.99 Other foremen (construction and related occupations not elsewhere classified)

Figure 5.2 Typical CODOT job categories and codes

371.05 Technical sales representative (industrial plant, machinery and equipment, excluding instruments)

Solicits orders for industrial plant, machinery or equipment (excluding instruments) the sale of which usually involves technical explanations and advice

Assesses the characteristics of the product to be sold, considering its technical capabilities and limitations, its cost and competitiveness in relation to similar products in the field; decides main selling points; maintains contacts with existing customers and develops contacts with new customers; explains product in lay or technical terms, highlighting those features most likely to appeal; advises on possible modifications which would make the product more acceptable to customer; quotes prices, credit terms and delivery conditions; records orders and arranges for delivery and/or installation of products sold, making follow-up visits as necessary to ensure customer satisfaction and to advise on technical matters and problems connected with the product; keeps abreast of all technical advances in his field; informs employer of any competitive advantages or weaknesses of product and suggests possible improvements. Performs these functions in relation to industrial plant, machinery and equipment excluding instruments.

May (01) rectify, or advise on the rectification of, defects in products sold

(02) attend on employer's stand at trade fairs, exhibitions, etc

(03) specialise in machine tools

(04) specialise in mechanical handling plant and equipment

(05) specialise in conveyor systems

(06) specialise in lifting gear

(07) specialise in earth moving equipment

(08) specialise in textile machinery

(09) specialise in printing machinery

(10) be responsible for a particular sales area, or superintend junior representatives and be known as Field sales manager or Superintendent (sales force).

Figure 5.3 Typical job description linked to CODOT code

722.02 Machine tool setter-operator (general)

Sets up and operates two or more types of machine tools such as lathes, milling machines, boring machines, grinding machines and drilling machines or a machining centre to cut, grind or otherwise shape workpieces

Ascertains job requirements from drawings and or other specifications; determines sequence and method of required operations; selects and fixes appropriate cutting or grinding tools; positions and secures workpiece on machine using jigs, shims, bolts, clamps and other positioning aids and fixing devices; sets machine controls for rotation speed, depth of stroke and cut, etc and adjusts machine table, stops and guides; operates automatic or manual control to feed cutting or grinding tool to workpiece or workpiece to cutting or grinding tool; checks accuracy of machining using measuring instruments; repositions workpiece, changes tools and resets machine as necessary. Performs these tasks in relation to the setting up and operating of two or more types of machine tool or a machining centre.

May (01) mark off workpiece prior to machining

(02) sharpen cutting tools

(03) set up and operate numerically controlled machine tools (722.36).

Additional factor: types of machine to which accustomed.

Figure 5.4 Typical job description linked to CODOT code

occupation. Although not exhaustive, these cover the majority of titles in use for the particular occupation.

Group and occupational definitions are also followed, where appropriate, by notes, cross references, inclusions and exclusions. Figures 5.3 and 5.4 show the detail given for two other positions.

Code numbers

A decimal system of code numbering is used. Minor groups are given code numbers of two digits within the range 00 to 99 and unit groups a code number of three digits within the range 001 to 999, the first two digits being those of the minor group to which the unit group belongs. Occupations are given two digits additional to the unit group number and separated from it by a point (.), so that occupational numbers consist of five digits. The following example illustrates this code numbering:

> Minor Group 31   Clerical occupations
> Unit Group 310   Supervisors (clerical occupations)
> Occupation 310.10   Supervisor (costing and accounting
>   clerical occupations).

Each minor group has provision for up to 10 unit groups and each unit group can accommodate up to 100 occupations.

Supervisory occupations are identified at unit group level within the code numbering system. All unit groups ending with a third digit of 0 relate to supervisors and foremen.

Fourth and fifth digits in the range .00 to .97 are used for specific occupations. The digits are allocated at intervals depending on the number of definitions to be accommodated. Trainees are given occupational numbers ending .98 within the unit group containing the occupations for which they are being trained. Trainee accountants are therefore classified 032.98. Residual occupations have an occupational number ending .99, e.g. 722.99 — other machine tool setter-operaters.

Special treatment is given to certain scientific, technical and managerial occupations so that all workers who have the same function or work with the same product or material can be readily identified. Each fourth digit is used to represent a specific functional characteristic, e.g. R&D, and each fifth digit to represent the field with which the worker is involved, e.g. heavy chemicals.

Job information

Users can add further digits to identify specific jobs within their own organisations, backed up as appropriate by standard job descriptions. It is important that job information used for coding and subsequent analysis should be properly maintained and up-to-date. Usually, this requirement is tied in with the company programme of job analysis and grading for remuneration purposes — a high motivator for keeping things up-to-date.

Job information covering all posts may be described as the building blocks for many management activities. Without job information, recruitment would be virtually impossible, training would have no target, salary administration would have no basis, organisation

structure and manpower planning would have no solidarity and the
activities of the methods and systems and work study staff would
be virtually impossible.

By 'job information' we refer to the essential parts of the job
which identify it and set it apart from other jobs. A job is built
round the requirement for the work necessary to achieve stated
objectives with known resources. The job information we require
will concern the function of a post, its content of duties and tasks,
the authority delegated to decide action and the potential effect
of action, responsibilities for assets and personnel. At a more specific
level, it will include responsibility for the achievement of specific
objectives or standards and the resources and time with which these
must be achieved.

It is not particularly difficult, within any company, to find out
what jobs people are holding. It is known who is called a chief
engineer and who is called a billing clerk and so on, but job titles
do not by any means tell the whole story. For example, the managing
director of a small organisation may operate his own production
machines and type his own letters, while I have known at least one
'technical assistant' who had considerable responsibilities for part of
a costly research and development programme.

Supervisory and management titles, in particular, seem to be
watered down in many companies. The old American joke about
the man who was made vice-president to forget his request for a
higher salary scale seems uncomfortably true — paper status does
have a value, and a bigger title costs less than a bigger salary.

Proper job information is, therefore, essential. Any exercise to
collect job information can reasonably be assumed to have applications
over the whole range of personnel activities, and may possibly have
other applications in addition. In other words, the information will
be required basically for job grading and salary administration and
for recruitment, but it will often have associated applications in the
training and personnel development fields, and also to organisation
planning. In companies which employ office methods specialists
and work study staff, job information in the clerical and production
areas may have applications in these functions also.

Application of job information

Application to salary administration   Job grading structures that
state job value relationships internally can only be built up from
basic job data on all the relevant factors. These vary from one job
family to the next, but include such items as responsibilities, effect
of decisions by the job holder, minimum educational and experience

requirements, and so on. This application is covered in detail later in this chapter.

Salary ranges attached to job grades provide a basis for determining individual salary levels (along with such other factors as job performance and potential ability). Job information is required in order to price each level.

Application to recruitment   The recruitment officer wants to know as much as possible about the type of man he has to find. The job specification should cover the requirements from an applicant in terms of his personality, his interests and motivation, and his education and experience. The recruiter is also concerned, but to a lesser degree, with the technical aspects of the work to be done, but his prime interest is in the employee specification.

Application to appraisal   The general manager requires a sound basis for appraising the performance of his subordinates. Job information for this purpose must get down to identifying real objectives to be attained in specific periods by using defined resources, so that subsequent appraisal is against as factual a background as can be achieved.

Application to training   The training manager is concerned with identifying the job skills which he has to teach. For the development of senior staff, he is interested in the job knowledge expected in the holder of a job, which he may be required to provide by training courses and test through planned assignments.

Once the full range of applications has been determined, the information requirements for each of these can be analysed thoroughly. It will be seen that information required for recruitment purposes varies from that required for, say, salary administration, which, in turn, is not the same as that required for organisation planning. However, from a widening range of applications there are clearly a number of factors that are common.

I have found that there is a great deal to be gained from making a very full analysis of the requirements for each of the planned applications. From this can be designed procedures that will collect all the data required for anticipated applications. Job information can be collected in a number of ways, from which two different approaches emerge.

In the first, a personal interview with the job holder is carried out by a job analyst or personnel officer to accumulate information which is then written up as a standard job description by the interviewer. Alternatively, carefully designed questionnaires may be used to obtain the information required quickly from the job holder and his manager.

The relative advantages of the two approaches are most simply summarised by saying that the interview method produces a higher standard of presented job information but is infinitely more expensive in terms of time and effort. My own experience in using both methods at different times is that the questionnaire method is effective and much to be preferred. The loss of standardised, but often stilted, quasi-legal descriptions which the interviewer tends to write is not vital. It is offset by the quality of the more lively writing of the job holder, which gives a better appreciation of the work. Regarding the time factor, the advantage of the questionnaire method is enormous, increasing the rate of production over that of the information collector at least tenfold.

The pace at which a study of this sort proceeds can vary very greatly. The only general comment one can make is that if a study is allowed to drag on for too long, the information obtained in the early stages is unlikely to match that obtained much later. Company organisation and jobs are changing steadily, even in what appears to be a static organisation. Information over 12 months old should be checked before use.

In a large organisation the questionnaire method may provide an across-the-board picture at one point in time which can be of substantial help during analysis of a fast-developing structure.

There is an almost infinite variety of forms in use. Most tend to be functional in that they are set out to fit specific applications and are not necessarily adaptable to other situations.

As one of the most important applications of job information is in job grading, one might expect some degree of standardisation here at least. However, the requirements of different types of evaluation schemes, such as points evaluation, factor comparison, or ranking, are different. In addition to the variations resulting from the use of different systems, the combinations of factor headings selected by different companies are also variable.

There is no ideal format for all situations, but Figures 5.5 and 5.6 show two of the better types of form in current use. Figure 5.5 is designed for use with a points evaluation scheme and gives special emphasis to structuring the description to provide clear-cut answers against each factor heading. Figure 5.6 is used with a ranking system and its range of headings is designed to cover all possible factors likely to influence relative job values.

To summarise, you can do no better than to analyse your immediate and longer-term needs from the data you are collecting, and then ensure that it is set out in the best possible way to provide ease of access for each potential application.

A logical development from a job information collection exercise is the preparation of a basic manual of standard descriptions. The format for these descriptions will normally be much simpler than

EXCELSIOR ENGINEERING COMPANY LTD.:
JOB INFORMATION RECORD

Job title:

Department:
Division:

Reports to:

Score summary

Factor	1	2	3	4	5	6	7	8	9	10	11	12	Total	Grade
Degree														
Score														

Part A:
Give a brief statement of the
function of the job

State briefly the major aspects
of the work

Figure 5.5 Job information record form: a type

PART B:
(Refer to the factor evaluation schedule before scoring each factor)

Factor 1: EDUCATION
What is the optimum education
required?

Factor 2: EXPERIENCE
What is the minimum period
of experience which the average
person would require?

Factor 3: SUPERVISION
Evaluate the degree of direction or supervision which the
job holder normally exercises

Factor 4: DECISIONS
Consider the responsibility of
the job holder for various
decisions

(Continuation not shown)

used for points evaluation with factor headings

JOB INFORMATION FORM

(This form should be completed by the person holding the position)

Name...

Job title ....

Organization ....

....

....

....

FOR SALARY ADMINISTRATION ONLY	
Job number	Job grade

Monthly/Weekly staff ....

Regular day work/Shift work ....

Normal hours (excluding overtime) ....

Approx. hours overtime to be worked per week ....

Description of duties: (Describe each duty clearly, defining the tasks which make up each duty. Start with the most time-consuming duties and finish with the minor duties. State whether the holder of this job directs or supervises the work of other employees and for what duties. In the column at the left state the approximate percentage of time normally spent on each duty.)

Percentage of time

(Signature of supervisor)..

Date......................

EDUCATION: What are the *minimum* technical, commercial or academic qualifications necessary for the proper performance of this work? For example G.C.E./O.N.C./H.N.C./University degree/etc. State subjects required.

EXPERIENCE: *In addition to the educational* qualifications defined above, what *minimum* experience is essential before appointment to this job?

SUPERVISORY RESPONSIBILITY: State the number and categories of employees supervised by the holder of this job. Where a section or larger organization is supervised an organization chart must be attached.

JOBS SUPERVISED	No. IN CATEGORY	JOBS SUPERVISED	No. IN CATEGORY

ASSETS AND MATERIALS: For what plant, machinery, tools, stock, valuables or cash, is the job holder responsible? State approximate value.

CONTACTS: Describe the purpose and frequency of personal contacts with others both within and outside the Company.

PLANNING AND DEVELOPMENT: What policies, plans, procedures, equipment or standards is the job holder responsible for initiating, developing, or improving?

DECISIONS: What decisions may the job holder take without reference to higher authority?

SUPERVISION RECEIVED: Describe the nature and frequency of direction and/or supervision received by the job holder.

(Signature of Department Head).. Date................

Exhibit 5.6 Job information form: questionnaire type for middle-level staff

the data collected for job grading, etc. It will aim at distilling the fundamentals of each post into a few crisp essentials. In use subsequently, 'Job coded 225.25' may be referred to, subject to stated variances, thus avoiding the need to prepare a complete new description.

Job families

Any form of job coding or job evaluation will draw attention to the way in which the various types of jobs tend to cluster into families, i.e. families of associated jobs such as chemical engineers, or cost accountants. As an illustration of this, it is not difficult to evaluate relative values within a series of accounting jobs, or within a group of development engineering jobs, but it is rather more difficult to tackle the evaluation of an accountant in relation to a design engineer. In other words, within job families, comparison and ranking are relatively straightforward, but between job families difficulties begin to arise. The reason is that within a family the range of factors is more constant — common scales of education and training requirements exist — and the question of assessing the importance of one factor against another does not arise.

Some job evaluation processes totally avoid the question of comparing jobs in one family with those in another, limiting their results to series of unrelated structures, each of which applies only to one job family. Where these small structures exist there can be no overall grading. However, the majority of grading structures still relate job values across all job families, accepting that this involves rather coarser standards of grading.

Changes of relationship within one family are easy to detect and the structure may be easily up-dated. Similarly, limited movement in market values affecting one family is easily acknowledged by adjusting the salary structure for that structure alone, without upheaval over the whole front.

Each and every job has its 'market value'. This value represents the salary that must be paid to attract and hold a fully competent individual who will perform the job at the required standard of effectiveness, taking all relevant factors into account. There may be (usually minor) variations in market rate which arise with locality, difficult working conditions, risk, work pace, and any variety of other possible requirements. Environmental factors of a more complex nature have an increasing impact on values as jobs rise into the executive levels.

If box engineers are in short supply, the various employers of such people will tend to offer higher salaries to attract any additional staff required, and may also raise the salaries of their existing people in order to retain them in the face of higher recruiting salaries offered by competitors. And so the market value rises. However, if similarly qualified people are attracted by this rising salary movement and switch to box engineering, the shortage is relieved, and the market value eases back towards its previous relationship with salaries of associated engineering staff categories.

Sometimes the availability of staff from associated groups is also limited. Where a flow of individuals cannot immediately take place to counteract the rising salary levels, the pressure is maintained and may result in a sharp rise in values. Further, where a shortage continues over a period of time, as has been the case with secretarial staff in the London area, the market rates may continue to edge up at above-average pace and move gradually out of line with previously accepted salary relationships. If the shortage continues, alternate methods of working may become economically sound and ease the demand.

By this process, the evolution of the ever-changing pattern of market values goes on continuously. Acceptance of this as an economic fact of life is fundamental to both job grading and salary administration. As the pattern reflects the economic situation of supply and demand, it can be 'bent' only marginally by local over-payment before a new value emerges.

5.4 Analyses of absenteeism and overtime

Analysis of absenteeism

The forms of absenteeism that we want to know about particularly, are those we may wish to do something about, such as absence which is unexplained, absence for sickness which sometimes appears exessive, and lateness. We also need to record absence for holidays for such things as jury service and for education — either part-time release or for examinations.

Control of absenteeism should fall wholly with local supervisors and managers, and they are also the source for much of the data which feeds into central records on absence. It may be that there is no problem; that the level of absence is tolerable and felt to be under control. Or, it may be that with absence running at above 15 per cent, we have had to adjust manning requirements upwards in order to man the equipment and ensure production, and that much of the absence is inadequately explained.

Our interest is likely to focus on the problem area, but to be sure we have a full measure of the problem, we need a report on the attendance of each employee, from which we can:

1   Assess the frequency of absence for each individual and the

total time lost by him over a defined period (of, perhaps, a year).

2   Analyse the reasons given; or lack of justification.

3   Determine the frequency and extent of lateness (although this is something which can be left entirely in the hands of competent supervision).

These analyses should provide us with a picture by department, clearly identifying the areas where absence tends to be high and also individuals with especially poor records. This information provides a basis for action.

The individuals with poor records may be chronically sick (and most larger companies have some such cases for much of the time). Is enough being done to rehabilitate or redeploy these people? There will also be a list of probable malingerers. More attention by the medical department may reduce their tendency to malinger, such as visits to their houses during absence to see if the treatment they are getting is adequate and medical examinations on return to work to ensure that they are fit. The casual excuse ceases to be so easy and only the deliberate case continues to insist on repeated absence with inexplicable pains in the head or back, etc. Insist on specialist investigation. Non-cooperation in dealing with a mutual problem may not be immediate grounds for dismissal, but extended over a long period, it may become justified.

Some of the habituals are likely to be in departments with particularly poor records. In most companies, these can be identified fairly readily before analyses are completed, for they will tend to be the departments with unpleasant working conditions and repetitive unsatisfying jobs.

A few years ago a government paper on absenteeism picked out 'providing maximum job satisfaction for all employees' as the major cause of action open to employers faced with high absenteeism. But how do you make a coal mine more attractive, and does it matter anyway when the miner says that he would only come in for three days a week if he could get enough money, that four days a week gives him enough, so why come in for five days and pay a lot more tax!

Not all jobs can be made more satisfying, as we know very well from many studies and literature. Some things can be done; frequently small things which have a surprising impact. Even tidying up and fresh paint says to employees that someone cares. Listening in carefully to the things discussed may provide pointers, but remember that the things that really cause distress and which employees assume cannot be altered will probably not come to the surface readily.

Many companies have attempted to reduce absenteeism and a lot have failed. As the cost of absenteeism is so high, and absenteeism trends are worsening, a permanent programme to draw attention

to the subject is necessary. The attention of management alone is
no longer enough. The facts should be on display in the departments
of serious concern, for the subject is of real concern to those work
people. They are the ones being absent, whose health appears poor.
And just what do they want to do about it?

We can leave the subject there. The analysis has been used to
highlight a problem, and perhaps to trigger action. Subsequent
reports will show any change in the trend, and investigations within
the department may lead to requests for additional analysis. The
initial objective has been met.

Analysis of overtime and part-time work

Manpower planning tends to assume that we are always dealing with
people who keep to the normal working week, and to do most of the
sums in 'equivalent full time' (EFT) manpower. This is an immediate
simplification and payroll numbers generally need correction to
relate total payroll with part-time employees into EFT manpower.

For complete logic, categories such as shift workers with regular
long hours need similar treatment. In a process plant with seven-day
continuous shift working averaging a 'basic' week of 56 hours per
man, a negotiated change to a 40-hour week gave a significant
increase in manpower for an unchanged volume of work. For a year
afterwards, the managing director had to explain this each time the
manpower figures were discussed, yet there had been no change in the
EFT manpower.

Overtime hours can be evaluated in a similar way, and frequently
are when redundancy is discussed. A 10 per cent cut in the number
of jobs may be offset by discontinuing the 10 per cent level of
regular overtime working — at least in theory. Good overtime control
is very important as the potential for wasting large amounts of
money is very high. Further, overtime hours carry premium payments
so that the manpower cost is higher than normal time rates, although
this may be offset by increased use of capital equipment.

Statistically, it is worth bringing to the attention of department
managers the costs of the overtime they are approving, together with
conversion into EFT manpower based on the number of hours
worked and on the costs including premium payments related to
basic earnings levels. This data becomes one of the factors in the
equation of getting additional employees to cope with a permanent
work load, or continuing to use overtime to overcome a temporary
peak. In looking at his short-term plan and utilisation of his people,
the manager will find the EFT manpower levels his most useful base.

Manpower models for use with computers provide a means of dealing with the large volume of data assembled (using sets of assumptions and probabilities) to show what would happen to the existing stock plus assumed intake needs to reach future manning requirements.

While many companies appreciate the value of fully computerised sales and profitability data, many less accept the need for processing manpower data in a similar fashion. In order to be able to assess manpower plans fully in an organisation of any size, the manpower information system needs to go to this newer level of sophistication.

Econometric model building is highly complex. Existing statistical data is analysed to seek out relationships between a wide range of variables, which may be defined in mathematical terms. Subsequently, a related series of equations is built up which shows the relationship between manpower requirements and other measures, usually using multiple regression analyses. The objective is not just to improve the validity of manpower forecasts, but rather to create a 'model' of the company that can be used to test the impact of various probabilities and show the impact on manpower requirements along with other factors.

Creating a model is an expensive and time-consuming business. Adapting limited-range models now available may prove of greater value. There are two main categories of model:

1   *The deterministic model* is the more simple of the two and is based on averages. It cannot show the probability of the forecast end result and oversimplifies both the situation and the forecast.

2   *The stochastic model* uses probabilities instead of averages and is substantially more complicated. It attempts simulation of real situations.

Given a highly sophisticated environment and a first-class manpower information system, the use of equally sophisticated models may provide a valuable additional input to the total manpower planning process. However, at the stage of development of the art at the time of writing, I consider model building and application to be on the experimental fringe of manpower planning practice. I expect to see substantial further development and use by the early eighties.

MANPOWER INVENTORY AND ANALYSIS

───────────────────────────────────────

Manpower supply to meet requirements can come from two sources. The preferred source is internal, but we need to know in detail the extent to which we can meet our requirements from the people employed already. If we find that the full requirement can not be found in this way, we shall need to resort to external sources. If it is find that we have numbers of people in certain categories who will become surplus to requirements, then time for retraining, redeployment or redundancy is needed.

To complete an assessment of our existing manpower resources in relation to our planned requirements, we need to take a careful inventory of our 'stock' in considerable detail and to analyse the changes taking place within. These will include such factors as the rates of progression through the structure on promotion and rates of loss.

6.1 The basic inventory

There is a series of activities that provide the necessary information on which to build our inventory:

1   An inventory of existing personnel sets out what we have in stock and can expect to have in stock at future dates. By setting these situations against requirements we have an immediate assessment of the shortfall.

2   Appraisal of existing performance supplements the inventory, telling us a great deal about the effectiveness of our present deployment of skills and identifying immediate needs.

3   Assessment of future potential also supplements the inventory

by adding a dimension. Against the pattern of change in future job requirements we have assessments of the rate and direction of individual development and the activity required to achieve this.

4   Assessment of manpower loss rates is also a vital part of this analysis as it is not very logical to plan the future use of manpower where, statistically, they are unlikely to be present in, say, three years! Loss rates of various categories and other relevant data must be assembled.

The basic manpower inventory does not consist of just one analysis, but of a large number of basic analyses which may be separate or cross-related. The more important aspects are covered below under appropriate headings.

Headcount

The most simple question is 'How many employees do we have?' The fact that there are x employees tells us very little. We need to know how many there are in each major piece of the organisation, in each department, and probably how many in each section. To make the picture anything like complete, we need a further break-down in the main employment categories — into hourly rated and staff; into other payment categories such as weekly paid staff, monthly, executive; into full time and part time; into direct and indirect; and, in spite of legislation, a breakdown into male and female is still useful.

Table 6.1 shows an extract from the manpower analysis summary prepared monthly for a large organisation. Other similar figures make comparisons with budgeted and forecast strengths, and changes from the previous month and year.

These reports represent the simplest form of stocktaking of employees, for as numbers change, we need to know something of the make up of the group and the way the mix may be evolving.

Qualifications, training and experience

A collection of people contains an accumulation of individual skills and abilities, and any inventory of an organisation's manpower needs to include a detailed analysis of these skills. What these skills consist of, and how they are used, represent two separate aspects which need to be reviewed separately.

At a first stage, this inventory may take the form of a summary of paper qualifications, and show the number of graduates, the number of ONCs, and so on. Further breakdown into the types and

TABLE 6.1 Manpower analysis report for month of June 1977*

Department	Total	Staff					Hourly rated		
		Male			Female		Male	Female	
		Executive	Monthly	Weekly	Monthly	Weekly		Full-time	Part-time
Clock production	161(-7)	1(-)	3(-)	17(+2)	1(-)	6(-2)	78(+2)	18(-2)	37(-8)
Purchasing	15(+1)	1(-)	4(-)	5(+1)	-	5(-)	-	-	-

* *Figures in parenthesis indicate net movement during month*

TABLE 6.2 Inventory of qualifications (abstract)

Qualifications	Total	Graduate level			Other	
		Post-grad.	1st/2nd Hons	Other	HNC	ONC
ARTS GRADUATES						
Languages:						
French	4	–	2	2		
German	1	–	1	1		
Russian	3	–	2	1		
Other	3	1	–	2		
Economics & political science	9	2	4	3		
Sociology, etc.	1	–	–	1		
Others (classics, history etc)	6	1	1	4		
TECHNICAL QUALIFICATIONS						
Mechanical engineering	29	–	2	2	17	8
Electrical engineering	28	1	2	1	13	11
Mech. & elect. engineering	4	–	1	–	1	2
Production engineering						

classes is usually necessary to separate the law graduate from the physics graduate, the electrical ONCs from the mechanical, honours from pass, and so on. Table 6.2 shows a summary of this sort which can easily be adapted for specific use in any situation.

It is worth taking considerable care over the coverage of qualifications as these are important pointers to the level and discipline of intellect, and it is likely that we shall wish to examine with care how we are using the skill we have.

Less easy to catalogue are all the other skills evolved from experience or less formalised training. In my experience, identification and coding of these skills is very difficult to do with accuracy, yet it will be from this data that many middle-management shortlists with be influenced, while our need to know how well we are using these skills may be as important as for graduates. The effort put into this identification and coding is likely to be determined in relation to the level of expected use and appreciation of the data assembled.

Since the development of industrial training on its present scale, recording of which people have been on which company training programmes, or major external courses, is important. The question of what happened to the course of '75 comes up regularly, together with similar questions about investments in expensive external training.

Present employment

How do we employ the people summarised on the company manpower report?

A simple form of analysis is of very limited value here. In any organisation, the variation in types of work undertaken involves the use of a substantial number of job-type categories for any meaningful breakdown. In a large company, some systematic basis for a detailed analysis is necessary, as a straightforward list of, say, 12 salesmen, 5 progress chasers, 17 export billing typists, 1 production manager, and so on, for several pages, would be confusing in the extreme. Some form of job family grouping is required as an interim stage.

All jobs can be fitted into a pattern of job families. These families link together jobs requiring similar training, experience and skills, so that individuals are better able to move to another post in the same family than to one in a different family requiring an unrelated range of skills. Job family groups include: Marketing, Personnel, Production Operations, Production Engineering, Clerical, Secretarial, and so on.

Each main family breaks down into series of sub-groups, each distinct in itself, but unmistakably part of the major family. For example, in the personnel family, sub-divisions would include: recruitment posts, training posts, industrial relations posts, and a further breakdown, for instance, into different types of training posts, is still possible before we reach individual jobs.

A straightforward decimalised coding system is generally used for analysis purposes in large organisations, often linked to personnel records on punched cards. This approach is easily adaptable to companies of any size.

The code numbers are built up according to the range of job categories and the degree of detail required. In a large organisation with many different jobs, number 123456 might be explained as follows:

12   The first two figures indicate the main job family — 'production'.
34   The second pair of figures cover sub-family coding, individual to each main job family; 12.34 is production control.
56   The third pair provides a further breakdown, which is individual against each set of figures from the first two sets, and enables each type of job to have an individual code number. 123456 is a scheduling supervisor.

The use of six digits provides a permutation of a million different numbers, although four rather than six digits are quite adequate in all but the largest companies. In practice, a company with 10,000 employees would not easily identify more than one-tenth of that number of different jobs, so that the number of code numbers actually required is not impossibly large.

The result of an analysis would show:

1   The numbers of people employed in each main job family.
2   The split into sub-families.
3   The numbers by different jobs, grouped meaningfully into families.

At least three significant job coding systems exist which we may choose to use instead of inventing our own. The most useful for normal manpower analysis is the CODOT system developed by the Department of Employment — primarily for their own use and therefore covering all types of employment from Cabinet Minister on down.* It is a five-figure coding in decimal form, supported by short definitions of the jobs covered in each category. For company use, the addition of two further digits could give a very fine breakdown to individual jobs if required.

Analyses by job category will be widely used. Although both initial coding and subsequent maintenance can be very time-consuming, this investment in effort is absolutely essential if subsequent analyses are to be of value.

Age distribution analysis

Actuaries are very fond of analyses of age distribution for pension

*See pages 105-109.

and life assurance funding appraisals. An analysis that shows the 129
overall age distribution, plus the scatter by types of people or by
departments, has much wider application. Study of such an analysis
can highlight the areas with age distribution problems. These may
arise wherever there is a clustering of any staff category into one
age group, with the potential situation of many people reaching
promotional readiness, or retiring age, in a short period, imposing
a strain on both succession planning and continuing effective
operation. Age-clustering at the younger level can mean restricted
promotion prospects, frustration and excessive loss of able staff.

I recall a study undertaken by one of the largest United Kingdom
organisations, which revealed that their overall age distribution varied
from the national age distribution. Analysis revealed that the
company's peaks were related to the intake of many younger people
at the times of rapid expansion.

The board of the company felt that an improved age scatter was
desirable, and that this might be achieved by tending to favour at
recruitment those people born during the company's 'off-peak'
periods. However, operationally this proved unrealistic.

This type of corrective action needs to be restricted to areas where
definite problems arise, rather than attempt to create an ideal
distribution which has little positive advantage. If a problem exists
or may develop due to age distribution, then it must be planned out
of existence.

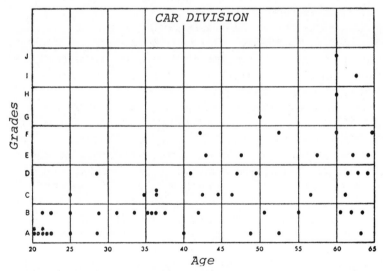

Figure 6.1 Age and grade distribution. (Note:
lack of younger men in the middle grades indicates
potential succession problems

With increasing numbers of younger men reaching high managerial positions at early stages, the age distribution with the management group of a company may provide pointers to difficulties. For example, if the directors of a company are all aged 35-40, then other staff in their 30's and 40's — and 50's — are likely to feel heavily restricted regarding prospects for further promotion. Few situations are as clear cut as this, of course, but a distribution of ages for each level of management may bring to light less obvious difficulties which can be given serious thought before they grow into problems.

Grade, rather than 'management level', provides a basis for finer analysis against age. Alternatively, salary may be substituted for grade. Gaps in the pattern may indicate potential succession problems, or too many close levels show clearly on the age versus salary graphs, indicating potential problems which require further investigation. However, the study may confirm an acceptable picture of relationships which present no apparent problems. Figure 6.1 shows a presentation of this data in which there are no obvious problems.

6.2   Inventory of performance appraisal data

Staff appraisal is well established as part of normal industrial life, although, looking at the great variety of appraisal methods, one sometimes wonders quite what is being achieved and quite what some managements think they are measuring. For our purpose here we need to have a basis for feeding into our manpower inventory information on performance and potential.

Appraisal covers two separate aspects of the employee at work. It is concerned first with how well he does his present job. Separately but complementarily, it is concerned with assessing his potential ability to do other work at the same level, or at a more senior level. This is covered later in this chapter.

The purpose of any performance appraisal plan is to provide a standard means for appraising how well the employee actually does the job for which he is employed. This assessment must start with a clear understanding of the job itself, the specific immediate and future objectives and of the time and resources allocated. This is not just an ideal state, but an absolute necessity which must be achieved if the appraisal is to be meaningful. The appraiser or rater must fully appreciate that he is appraising the man against the job, and that any factors not associated with performance of the job are irrelevant.

It is also essential for the appraisal to be carried out by trained management who appreciate the difficulties of the task they undertake. Bias, attributable to lack of appreciation of these points, may produce high ratings for senior people and low ratings for junior people, which the manager will justify by quoting a straight comparison between one of his senior supervisors and one of his clerks, making the obvious statement that 'the supervisor is doing much more than the clerk'. Such a 'rating' obviously contains a combination of performance and job value and its value is very limited until the two factors can be identified and examined separately.

As an example of the appreciation of finer points which the appraiser must have, consider a buyer who purchases all the requirements of a unit, his purchases being valued at, say, £500,000 a year. He may or may not be the final arbiter in respect of price and conditions associated with these purchases. The rater must know the answer to this question before he can effectively appraise this job holder's performance of his job, for the judgement and negotiating skill required may be substantially influenced.

Questions of this sort are not peculiar to senior posts. To what extent is the work of a clerk accepted, or checked, by a more senior clerk? Is accuracy his own, or someone else's, final responsibility?

Of course, jobs are constantly evolving and precise job information is not always available. While some companies will have a full up-to-date library of written job descriptions, other organisations accept a situation of constant and irregularly recorded job information. In either situation, a brief discussion and verbal agreement on the current position provides a sensible introduction to any appraisal.

Management by objectives (the style of management which uses objectives-setting as a basis for planning and control) exists in some form in virtually every company that has detailed business planning. The defined commercial objectives, with their timing and statement of resources required, provide the milestones for checking off progress and achievements.

Extensions of these commercial objectives, again linked to time scales and resources, state the roles that individual managers and senior staff must play in achievement of the total plan. It is these objectives which provide the starting point for appraisal of individual performance. As an activity, this has to be undertaken in relation to the total business plan.

It is virtually essential that individuals should participate in the preparation of their personal objectives and accept them as realistic.

An efficient appraisal system is not dependent solely on the annual written report. In the right environment there is likely to be ongoing discussion throughout the year between manager and subordinate, often at an informal level around particular points as they arise. This situation is indicative of good personal relationships and good management attitudes, but does not replace the need for periodic, formal 'summing-up', which will provide the basis of our inventory of performance appraisal data.

The part that appraisal plays in management manpower planning is substantial. The main point is that individuals moving up a promotional ladder are likely to leave a sequence of successful assignments behind them. And, in looking back at any man's career, the manager examining past appraisal reports is likely to look for this success story. It is very much easier for him if scored reports are already interpeted and he can see at a glance how they stand against those of other staff on comparable jobs; or where he can read through a written summary of achievement against targets.

6.3   Inventory of potential ability data

'What other jobs could this employee do now?' 'What jobs should this employee be able to do in future, given proper training and the opportunity to develop experience?' Answer these questions fully and accurately and there is little more to the appraisal of an employee's potential.

The difficulty is, can these questions be answered? And if they can, by whom, and in what form? Of all the aspects of appraisal, one man's view of another's potential is likely to be the most inaccurate. It is especially open to bias, and even rational attempts may consist of unrealistic statements and suggestions, due to lack of adequate knowledge of situations or appreciation of the make-up and requirements of jobs. For example, complete reliability at the simple skills of addition and subtraction will not automatically make a good accountant; and a chief engineer needs more than an engineering degree and design ability.

A classic example of the difference between known performance and potential occurred when a high-calibre graduate doing a stint as a trainee in the personnel department was assigned to the personnel records section for two weeks to get to know the work. He picked up the entire operation in a couple of days, but was given records clerical work to do. Bored, he made appalling blunders while his mind was on other things and was clearly useless as a records clerk. But his ability to run a complete personnel department within a year or so was undoubted — and subsequently proven.

The senior clerk in the same records section, who had his routine job completely under control, was given a small promotion, but had to be relieved of his new post a month later as it proved to be beyond him. Potential ability does not necessarily co-relate with performance on present work.

Both assessment and inventory of potential must acknowledge that:

1   Each employee is likely to be changing steadily and some will be growing rapidly in capacity towards readiness to take bigger jobs.

2   Assessments of potential will be reliable for only two or three years ahead and for only one career step beyond present position.

An inventory of stored materials reflects a stock position which is reasonably stable (although some may deteriorate and other stock may become obsolete). An inventory of people, and particularly of performance appraisal and potential, is far more dynamic. Last year's data is of interest, but it is only the latest picture which tells the story we need for current action and decisions. These tell what his weaknesses and strong points are; his motivation, ambitions and the limitations he accepts; together with an assessment of his response to new situations and general development. On this base, an assessment of further potential develops.

Which of our employees has potential for significant career advance within a reasonable period? Appended to many performance appraisal forms is a short final section directed at the employee's overall suitability for other work. For all those staff considered to have any potential for advancement, there will be further questions in another form. Figure 6.2 shows a typical tail-end question from

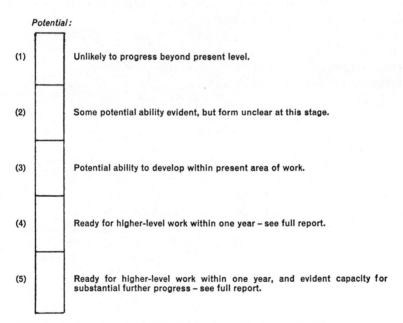

Potential:

(1)   Unlikely to progress beyond present level.

(2)   Some potential ability evident, but form unclear at this stage.

(3)   Potential ability to develop within present area of work.

(4)   Ready for higher-level work within one year – see full report.

(5)   Ready for higher-level work within one year, and evident capacity for substantial further progress – see full report.

Detailed reports are to be prepared for all employees in categories 4 and 5.

Figure 6.2   Short report on potential (appended to performance report)

the performance rating of a major engineering company — an opening gambit to a further questionnaire and useful data for inclusion in our inventory.

These opening questions can be assumed to weed out the 'non-starters' effectively. Over-estimation of future potential is a widespread fault. It is comparatively rare for any individual to be marked below his realistic level. There is, therefore, no advantage in covering all staff by detailed questionnaires on potential.

Having short-listed those individuals considered able to progress beyond their present levels during the next five years a standard approach is necessary so that assessments done at different times and places by different people may be realistically compared and found meaningful.

Potential ability is too ephemeral a thing, too easily assessed wrongly and too easily reported inadequately for us to make reporting a cold, formal act. If assessments are to be alive and have value and meaning, it is essential that they should be built up in discussion. This discussion, and the formal reporting, should be carried out be an individual experienced and effective in the use of interviewing techniques, and sufficiently able to command the respect of those he interviews to obtain a full and considered appraisal of each employee discussed. The obvious choice is the individual responsible for management manpower planning, subject to a limit of maybe 200 personnel.

The prime question is: 'What other posts do you think he is capable of filling?' To avoid a glut of future managing directors, this question must be qualified in a number of ways and associated with questions on timing and training.

6.4   Inventory of psychological assessment data

With the growing use of psychological tests for many aspects of selection, it is logical that this data should become part of our total manpower inventory. It is equally important that data of such a highly sensitive nature should be protected and remain confidential. Not only is the carrying out of psychological testing a specialised professional activity, but the interpretation of the end results should always be handled in the same way. Those who think otherwise might consider submitting to surgery at unskilled hands — a reasonable analogy. Hence, the use of many techniques is restricted to professional psychologists who, in all but the largest organisations, may be employed in an external service organisation on a retainer basis in much the same way as a patent agent or solicitor.

The psychologist is interested in the many separate aspects of an individual's make-up and personality. Take 'intelligence' as an example; this breaks down into a number of individual aspects. An employee's verbal abilities may be quite unrelated to his arithmetic ability. There are many finer aspects and the psychologist may be interested in any group or combination depending on the proposed employment of his candidate. Similarly, 'personality' builds up from a multitude of aspects, many of which the psychologist may assess. Mental balance and reactions under stress are parts of this picture and provide valuable aids to the executive selector. The more that is known about an individual, the less likelihood of error. Career planning for executive staff frequently includes results from series of psychological tests which are used as a cross-check on other data and to cover the ground in greater depth.

The proper use of a battery of standard intelligence tests provides a cross-check on educational achievement by drawing attention to apparent oddities in the relationship between normal test scores for people with the claimed examination result level and the actual scores of the individual. The difference between an individual's test results and usual scores for people with the degree he claims will often identify a man who falsely claims a qualification at a recruitment interview. As a further example, tests may confirm an ability in, say, pure mathematics, but add the information that there is a lack of ability in practical application; or show some other combination of skill and inability.

Intelligence test and tests of simple basic skills and abilities are primarily used as part of selection procedures and have applications to both potential recruits and to established staff. There are obvious advantages in making as many cross-checks as possible before recruiting a new employee, particularly if the post is a senior one. There is also considerable value in using tests on employees who are to be redeployed or who may be redundant. By this means, potential skills or abilities may be uncovered that greatly enhance potential employability and which might otherwise have remained unknown and dormant.

Intelligence cannot really be measured as an entirety. It is made up of a number of pieces. Most intelligence tests are designed to assess one piece only, e.g. verbal, arithmetical, or logical thinking ability. Even these tests of strictly limited range cannot be considered accurate as the yardsticks are not definable in any way comparable with bases for measuring, say, distance or weight. The best a test can do is to take some of the known information about the aspect concerned, set up a questionnaire around this information and then collect results from a large population. The distribution of results from this wide trial provides standards against which any individual score may be considered.

This apparently rather crude approach is systematically and statistically sound, but it is necessary to emphasise that psychological results must be interpreted skilfully. While all psychological tests require professional interpretation, some of the more simple material for measuring facets of intelligence only may be used by trained 'testers' working remote from the specialist, provided they keep strictly within defined limits of interpretation.

Personality tests are used to provide a profile of the personality of a candidate, covering a series of personality factors. Probably the most commonly used is the 16PF, which covers sixteen factors, and has been validated for considerable variety of population and employment groups, which give substantial authority to test results and conclusions. The end results of the 16PF are displayed as a 'profile'. The individual scores are shown between definitions of the extremes of each scale, together with the percentage of scores normal at each level. The extent to which an individual deviates from population norms is immediately visible, together with any relatively uncommon characteristics. Similarly, an individual profile can be examined against a norm for his employment group and the significance of substantial variations considered.

There are other products of these tests, which may lead to the use of further investigatory tests. One example is that vulnerability to stress may be indicated. If the candidate is to be placed in a post where stress will be high at times, the need to know more about his stress tolerance, and therefore suitability for the post, is very important. I have heard this type of examination criticised as probing too far into private aspects of an individual, but having seen at least one individual avoid being placed in a situation which would have led inevitably to a nervous breakdown in 3-6 months, I need no further justification.

A second example is that strong tendencies to mental unbalance may be indicated. While this may not rule out the candidate for consideration, for jobs where this level of testing has been required, such a tendency should be carefully assessed by the psychologist involved.

There can be interpretation of these tests by suitably trained laymen, but these interpretations cover basics only. The finer points remain fully under the control of the psychologist, and his diagnosis must be treated with the same care and confidentiality as personal medical history.

The rates of loss of existing staff are important factors in manpower planning. The fact of loss is important to the company in that each individual who leaves takes a knowledge of the company and of his job which can rarely be acquired ready-made from outside. The impact of turnover is reduction from full efficiency, at least for a period, even when a new appointment is made immediately.

It is important to the company to know and understand its manpower turnover situation. To begin to do this it must understand the character and mix of its workforce, for any overall 'turnover index' will be useless. It is essential to go into detail, to be aware of the loss rates for each type and category of staff, and to assess those figures in relation to the current population in each category. For example, a high proportion of recent recruits is likely to mean higher than 'average' turnover.

Manpower turnover seems to follow reasonably clear patterns which make it possible to forecast probable future loss rates for most categories. In general, most types of manual worker have a high early loss rate. People decide very quickly that they do or do not like the company or their supervisor or something else, and leave almost immediately. If they have come into a training programme, the fall-out rate may be very high in the first days; then weeks. The first few days, then, are critical. If the man can be encouraged to settle immediately, he may stay for life. If not, he will look elsewhere immediately. Statistical analysis produces a picture (see Figure 6.3) showing the heavy loss rate during the

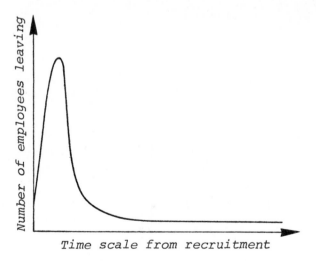

Figure 6.3 Typical pattern of loss rates of semi-skilled employees

Table 6.3 Analysis of staff turnover (extracts)

i. Analysis by categories:

Job category	Average strength during year	Terminations in year		Termination % for previous year	Number transferred or promoted from category
		Number	% of average strength		
Female staff:					
A. Secretarial					
(1) Secretaries	7	2	29	33	—
(2) Shorthand typists	12	7	58	55	2
(3) Copy typists (inc. billing, etc.)	27	18	67	76	1
(4) Other	4	2	50	25	—

ii. Analysis by reasons for leaving:

Reason	Primary reason		Primary + contributory	
	Number	Proportion of total	Number of mentions	Proportion of total
Male staff:				
Salary and benefits	4	14%	21	18%
Promotion prospects	7	24%	15	13%
Under-employment	2	7%	9	8%
Generally dissatisfied	3	10%	14	12%
Domestic reasons	2	7%	3	3%

iii. Summary
Turnover figures are slightly down on the previous year for female staff, but slightly up for males. This reflects some reduction in the rate of industrial growth locally, but movement of a number of good young men to other areas.
Loss of young men is associated directly with feelings of lack of promotion and salary prospects, as brought out at interview. These reasons were given by men in the 20-30 age group more than twice as frequently as for male staff as a whole; a more detailed study is in progress.
Analysis of past performance by leavers indicates ....

initial period, and then reduction to a plateau of steady slow loss. Once proven as the norm for a category, it can be applied directly to forecasting future loss rates for that category and taken into account in recruiting programmes. But be careful if you ease up on recruitment, for shortly afterwards, your pace of losing employees from the category will also ease up as there are few very short-service employees.

Termination patterns vary for different categories. As we move up into clerical and technical categories, losses from very short-service groups are relatively rare (the individuals not liking to show very quick changes in their personal histories), but at 1½-2½ years there is a peak. At this point, there can be a reasonable claim to have completed a job well and be seeking new opportunities. Careful analysis may show up a second, lower peak at about 3-4 years, coinciding with completion of a second job. After this, the varying length of job cycles gradually smooths out into a progressively lower loss rate. This same pattern is much the same up through the executive levels of the company, for there too, there can be a claim of successful completion of assignment at 1½-2½ year intervals.

Table 6.3 shows extracts from an analysis which provides a valuable aid to planning in one company. By indicating the factors influencing turnover, from carefully run interviews with those about to leave, the analysis provided a basis for estimating future trends and taking action to alter those trends. Depending on the findings, those factors may include the need to change company salary levels and benefits, or alter supervisory or company style to make the working environment more attractive.

In one study I made between two neighbouring and near-identical plants, it was the one with the higher pay levels which had much the higher turnover levels. Investigation showed substantial differences in supervisory style with heavy handed, authoritarian supervisors virtually driving good employees out of the door and blaming 'low wage levels' for their plight.

In making calculations of future loss rates, normal retirements may be treated separately as they are, of course, certainties. Statistically calculated loss rates for all other employees can be built up gradually, together with trend lines, and become progressively more meaningful and useful. From these analyses, we can make forecasts of expected loss rates with increasing accuracy, given sufficient detail of existing employees in the categories of interest.

The formula most generally used to express turnover is:

$$\text{Annual manpower turnover} = \frac{\text{Leavers over 12 months}}{\text{Average manpower over same period}} \times 100$$

As appropriate, the rates can be worked out on data for a month or a quarter, but these may be affected by short-term fluctuations. A running average based on the latest quarter is probably best if you are keeping an urgent watch on a situation; with the reminder that the data for employees with short service will produce different figures from data covering long-service employees, in most categories.

Another valuable way of presenting manpower turnover is to change the emphasis from the negative one of 'who has gone' to the positive approach of 'who has stayed'. Survival rates have to be based on intake 'cohorts' — groups of employees who joined the organisation at roughly the same time and in the same category.

No turnover analyses have much to comment on the one-off — who either stays or goes. But bring in fifty trainee assemblers, a quarter on a regular basis, and efforts to improve the survival rate by better selection and training can be clearly seen (see Figure 6.4). A calulation used in association with this approach is to measure the half-life of the category. How long do we manage to retain at least 50 per cent of the intake? If that period is short and can be extended, this can be financially significant.

Age may be a factor in loss rates for some categories. Older recruits may tend to be more stable. A simple age service scattergraph of the category under review will highlight this quickly, and may point to an improvement in the recruitment specification. I have seen this occur with semi-skilled assemblers, where the loss of women under 30 was nearly three times the loss rate for older women. By limiting intake to the older group, the loss rate was minimised.

The age versus grade distribution of losses, compared with the total company age versus grade picture, may show that a high proportion of the younger men in the higher grades are leaving. Such a finding would indicate heavy losses of high-calibre people and clearly should lead to a closer study. A straightforward age x salary comparison may be used to check this same point. Figure 6.5 illustrates this and also highlights one of the reasons — a heavy population of older staff blocking promotional channels.

Parallel analyses may show proportionately heavy losses from various staff groups, some of which are likely to be known, but others may have been unsuspected. Identification is the first step towards turning on the spotlight and attacking the problem.

6.6 Analysis of promotion patterns

A series of analyses, each covering movement into and out of a single grade and category of manpower over a period of time, will enable a statistical picture of normal rates of promotion and

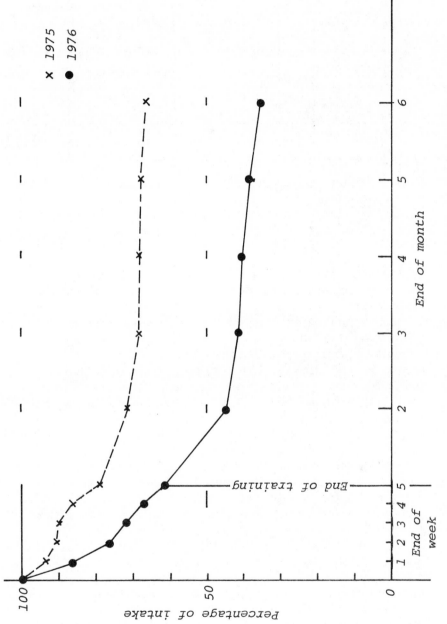

Figure 6.4 Survival rate of trainees, for two years

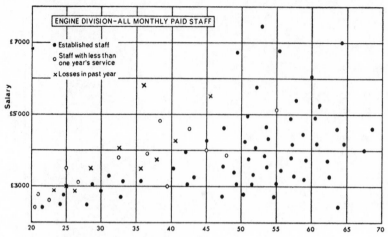

Figure 6.5 Age and salary distribution, showing turnover

other changes to be built up — defining the 'flows' through the function selected, subject to the conditions prevailing during the study period.

The raw data required starts in the form set out in Table 6.4 which covers the function selected and the various levels and categories of manpower within the function. If there are several departments in different divisions or subsidiaries, these should be analysed separately to ensure that varying local conditions do not produce differing pictures. Following the overall analyses, a whole series of subsidiary analyses should follow, examining the groups by age, by qualification, by length of time in the grade or category, and by various combinations of these factors.

From this data, we can build up a set of statistical norms based on past experience. Table 6.5 shows an analysis of the probability of promotion for a category of engineer — in one company, given a particular set of circumstances. This is one of a series of analyses covering the various engineering categories in the study.

The value of this analysis is limited by the assumption that the opportunity for flows will continue at the previous rate. If there is any significant change of circumstance and 'throughput', the assumptions on promotion opportunities will be changed.

If the 'norm' percentages of engineers ready to move into higher positions cannot be accommodated, the result is not a simple slowing up of promotion. The engineers ready for promotion are likely to react by seeking other opportunities and the reduction in internal

Table 6.4 Analysis of manpower movement in engineering department

Category	Strength 1 January	Promotion from (1 grade)	Promotion from (2 grades)	Transfer to other Divisions	Leavers	Total movement	% of total	Promotion to (1 grade)	Promotion to (2 grades)	Transfer from other Divisions	Recruits	Strength 31 December
Managers	6	1	-	-	1	2	33%	1	1	-	-	6
Senior Engineer I (Supervisors)	8	1	-	1	1	3	37%	1	1	-	-	7
Senior Engineer II	10	1	1	1	1	4	40%	2	1	-	1	10
Engineer I	21	2	1	-	3	6	29%	8	-	1	2	26
Engineer II	37	8	1	1	6	16	43%	8	-	-	10	39
Assistant Engineer	14	8	-	-	1	9	64%	-	-	-	8	13

Plus further analyses by age groups, qualification levels, years of service in grade, etc.

Table 6.5 Engineer I: probability of promotion within one year

Service in grade	Age				
	21-23	24-26	27-30	31-40	41 and over
Up to 1 year	12%	15%	9%	-	-
1 year and up to 2 years	21%	30%	28%	15%	-
2 years and up to 3 years	-	38%	30%	10%	-
3 years and up to 5 years	-	12%	18%	16%	8%
5 years and up to 1o years	-	-	7%	12%	8%
10 years and over	-	-	-	10%	-

promotions is likely to be offset by an equivalent increase in the rate of losses to outside organisations.

Data on promotion patterns is invaluable as an input to manpower supply planning in that it quantifies the probabilities on your ability to provide the required numbers from internal promotion, category by category. Equally, this analysis will quickly highlight where promotion potential cannot be absorbed and higher turnover may be expected.

If future promotion requirements are greater or less than previous experience, some actions are possible to contain this, provided the situation is recognised early enough. For example, if the requirement will increase, what can be done to upgrade the stock from which promotions will come — to increase the numbers of people in the high promotion rate categories. Referring to Table 6.5, can we increase the numbers aged 24-26 with 1-3 years' service by more selective recruiting? In contrast, if the promotion opportunities are likely to decline, it is probably worth adjusting our recruiting to take in more 30-40 year olds, who will ensure stability and retention of knowledge, without high promotion expectations.

Normal career projection lines may become much clearer from these analyses, with obstacles and bottlenecks identified so that arrangements can be made for their removal. Loss analyses may reveal part of the story, by showing heavy losses of people at one grade level in a function, perhaps due to a gap in the structure and with intake to higher grade levels. Promotion pattern analysis would show the absence of reasonable promotion flow through the level in question, pin-pointing the problem more precisely.

One manpower group where promotion flow analysis is particularly important is that of the graduate intake. All too frequently, the loss rates of graduates after 2 or 3 years with the organisation tends to make nonsense of the expense and efforts to recruit them from universities to fill future supervisory, managerial and specialist positions. The reasons for losses may become much more apparent when the flow analysis shows a lack of promotion opportunities into suitable positions because they are too young and inexperienced. But remember that these analyses only identify the problem. They do not alter attitudes or increase promotion opportunities. The action plan must be designed separately and implemented.

MANPOWER SUPPLY PLANNING

Our planning must focus on optimising our use of manpower resources.

7.1 Identifying manpower supply action required

This section starts from the two assumptions that we have:
1   A clear picture of forward manpower requirements, in 'exploded' form, to show detail by function, category and level at a series of points in time.
2   A clear picture of our current manpower inventory, also in 'exploded' form using the same breakdown by function, category and level and to which we have applied the knowledge we have of the ways in which existing manpower is developing, being promoted, or learning. This should also be summarised at the same points in time.

    Our task starts with overlaying requirements with available supplies and analysing the differences; taking parts of the organisation and functions piecemeal in view of the likely complexity of the whole.

    The resulting pictures are likely to show a great range of mismatch situations, with an excess in some categories, skills and levels, and short supply of others. The remainder of our task will be to determine the extent to which we can bring the two parts together by modifying both our requirements and our stock, by means of retraining and redeployment to shift any excess of manpower into short-supply areas.

    More than anywhere else in this book I recognise the need for

actual examples to illustrate the form analyses can take at this
stage of planning and the rest of this section is allocated to a series
of examples and associated commentary, ranging from simple,
single-department, short-term plans, through to extracts of critical
areas in company five-year plans.

Table 7.1 shows a summarised analysis of requirements taken
from actual papers covering one particular department, the summary
being shown in the form of a balance sheet of existing and required
personnel.

1   On the left-hand side of the sheet, the first column shows the
    various types of jobs that exist within the department.
2   The next column shows the number of posts — the present
    position.
3   Subsequent columns show the anticipated losses from each
    category of staff, and the anticipated numbers to be transferred
    or promoted from each category.
4   A further column shows the 'plus' of transfers and promotions,
    including some from the previous column, but some from
    other departments, as any plan of this sort must anticipate
    interdepartmental movement.
5   The net figures from the early columns then appear, showing
    anticipated change in the existing staff application.
6   The last two columns show the new staff total at the end of
    the forecast period, and the balance required to make up the
    existing total to the new total.
7   The 'balance required' column contains the key set of figures,
    and shows against each of the types of jobs the number that
    will be required during the period of the forecast. In one
    category, the analysis shows that over-staffing must result
    owing to a run down in the number of billing clerks required.

These detailed analyses become the work plans for the following
stage of planning the recruitment of staff required. As a generalisation,
we should aim to meet as much of our requirement from existing
supplies as possible. It is normally less expensive and has a considerable
impact on retaining the best people as they can see that internal
promotion is a reality.

The requirement plan, if it is to be effective, needs to contain
more than simply the categorised manpower levels at the beginning
and end of a one-year period and the calculated requirement for
the period. For the immediate short-term future, say, for a minimum
of six months and possibly up towards two years, it is desirable to
develop the plan in sufficient detail for anticipated requirements to
show on a month-by-month basis.

Figure 7.1, which is the development of Table 7.1, shows the
phasing of manpower required by a department, broken down on
a month-by-month basis. This particular example shows the

Table 7.1 Departmental one-year manpower requirement forecast

Types of jobs	Number of staff required	Anticipated loss		Anticipated gain transfer/promotion	Net	Total requirement forecast at......	Balance required during year
		Terminations	Transfer/promotions				
Department manager	1				1	1	-
Cost accountant	1				1	1	-
Billing supervisor	1				1	1	-
Accounting operations sup'r	1		1*	1	1	1	-
Assistant accountant	1			1	2	2	-
Cashier	1				1	1	-
Book-keeper	2		1		1	2	+1
Accounting operations clerk	6	2	1	1	4	6	+2
Billing clerk	5	1			4	5	+1
Records clerk	2	1			1	2	+1
Filing clerk	1				1	1	-
Secretary	1				1	1	-
Shorthand typist	2	1			1	2	+1
Billing typist	5	2			3	5	+2

*To HQ Department

requirement at each stage and, on the right-hand side, shows the
normal induction/training period, i.e. the period that an employee
should be in a post, or at least in the company, before he can be
expected to be effective. This provides a guide to the entry or
induction date for additional employees whether recruited or
transferred.

It involves the selection of sources of each category of staff in
terms of where these people are to come from; planning how they
will be obtained; what training or development or induction they
will need before they will become effective; and so on. From this
exercise, an overall recruitment and training operating plan can
be evolved.

In a short-term plan this involves scheduling the recruitment of
the various staff required, taking into account any time necessary
to define the post, prepare and publish any advertisement, sort and
interview candidates, select the most able and perhaps negotiate
terms, and then wait while notice is worked before he joins. The
times will vary for a number of reasons, e.g. the ease or difficulty
of attracting suitable candidates and the differing lengths of notice
required. The result is that, with varying periods of induction to
allow for, initiation of a recruitment campaign may need to begin
anything from three weeks up to a year before an individual is
required to become effective.

Table 7.2 covers an applications engineering department over
a period of five years. Of particular interest is that this company
chose to build up its assessments of future manning requirements

Job title	Action
Accounting operations supervisor	Jenkins marked for promotion to HQ in April. Accounting operations clerk Patteson to replace him
Assistant accountant	Promotion of Salmon to new post - September or October
Book-keeper	Replacement for Salmon - recruit July onwards
Accounting operations clerk	Three replacements anticipated. Plan intake of one from training course September. Recruit as required
Other categories	Recruit as required

Figure 7.1 Notes on detailed phasing of forecast

Table 7.2 Manpower requirements forecasts (extract from working sheet)

Job category	Strength at 1.1.1976	Forecast strengths – 5-year forecast								End 1979	End 1980	End 1981	Notes
		1977				1978							
		End 1st qtr.	End 2nd qtr.	End 3rd qtr.	End 4th qtr.	End 1st qtr.	End 2nd qtr.	End 3rd qtr.	End 4th qtr.				
Applications engineering department:													
Manager	1	1	1	1	1	1	1	1	1	1	1	1	
Head – customer service	1	1	1	1	1	1	1	1	1	3	3	3	Regional breakdown 1979
Head – application research	–	–	1	1	1	1	1	1	1	1	1	1	Vacancy advertised
Head – applications library	–	–	–	–	–	–	–	1	1	1	1	1	Part of regionalisation plan
Senior engineer	7	7	8	8	9	9	9	10	10	15	15	15	F/C on work analysis
Applications engineer (a)	18	19	20	21	22	23	24	25	26	30	34	38	(a) Ratio-trend F/C (not used)
(b)	18	18	20	20	22	24	26	29	34	35	42	50	(b) F/C on work analysed
Research engineer													
Technical assistant (a)	20	21	22	23	24	25	26	27	28	32	36	40	(a) Ratio-trend (not used)
(b)	20	20	20	18	18	18	18	20	20	22	24	26	(b) Work analysed F/C used

Etc.

on two bases, and did not subsequently confirm either one. Using current ratios of work volumes to manpower required produces very different conclusions to analysis of expected work and conversion to requirements. In this case, the type of work is expected to change, and work analysis indicates that the technical requirements will be generally higher than with current work, which is not evident from following a trend line on current ratios.

Table 7.3 covers a subsidiary company within a building group, which set out its current position and five-year forecast without showing the year-to-year detail, which was added later. The objective was to get a view of the longer-term implications of their growth plans while ignoring short-term fluctuations expected along the way.

As the subsidiary is structured with four sub-units, some of which have branch offices, the opening actuals show a breakdown, not shown at the five year stage. A volume growth of the order of 30 per cent was anticipated.

The loss rates currently being experienced by the company were very high and, even with some reduction from present levels, the impact of losses on the need to train and develop several categories is severe. For example, losses of foremen will not be offset by the planned training programme by a very wide margin although the number of trainee/assistant foremen will be almost trebled.

This points strongly to a need to review the calibre of the intake and the content of the training in order to speed up the throughput and retention of new formen. The next update of the plan will, hopefully, reflect an improved picture, but only if the problem now identified is considered to have been solved.

The creation of intake categories of surveyors, estimators and buyers is in response to shortages of these groups, but again, the expected loss rates and the duration of trainee/assistant periods make this tactic look of doubtful value. A revised programme to bring in individuals capable of responding to speeded-up training and development may produce a far more satisfactory end result; lower headcount, lower costs, lower loss of skills, less frustration for the established skilled people, and an earlier supply cf competent support staff.

An alternative form of presenting the build up of staff by function over a two-year period, showing the detailed timing of requirements, has already been shown in Table 4.1. This form is valuable in setting out the timing of requirements but that value is limited by lack of data on specific categories, and allowance for loss rates. For example, a build up of production employees is likely to be accompanied by high initial loss rates and the volume of recruitment necessary to achieve a force of 16 might be twice that number over the eighteen-month period.

Table 7.3 Building group manpower requirements areas

Category	End 1977 actuals					End 1982 forecast total		Estimated loss rates inc retirement		Estimated promotions required		Estimated requirement from outside group	
	Company A	B	C	D	1977 Total	Inc	Total	%	Total over 5 years	Promotion from	Promotion to	Total over 5 years	Aver. annual rate
MD/Manager	1	1	2	1	5	−1	4	—	1	—	—	—	—
Branch Manager	—	—	1	—	1	3	4	—	1	—	2	2	2
Chief Contr Mgr/Dir	1	1	—	—	2	—	2	—	—	—	—	—	—
Contract Managers	8	5	3	3	19	+3	22	10%	10	1	3	11	2
Foremen	13	12	20	—	45	+10	55	20%	50	3	20	43	9
Trainee/Asst Foremen	11	7	3	3	24	+41	65	20%	44	20	—	105	21
Chief Surveyor	1	1	2	1	4	—	4	10%	2	—	2	—	—
Surveyors	10	8	3	1	22	3	25	15%	18	2	12	11	2
Asst/Trainees	—	—	1	—	1	11	12	20%	6	12	—	29	6
Chief Est/Plnrs/Buyer	2	2	2	—	6	2	8	10%	3	—	2	3	1
Est/Plnrs/Buyers	—	4	4	2	10	4	14	15%	9	2	4	9	2
Asst/Trainee Est/Plr/Buyer	1	—	—	—	1	11	12	20%	6	4	—	21	4

Table 7.4 Civil engineering group – manpower survey – five years 1975–79

Category	Present strength	Immediate requirements	Current proposed strength	Resignations & retirements anticipated	Promotions from staff	Additional requirements					Strength 1979
						1975	1976	1977	1978	1979	
Managing Director	1					1					1
Contracts Director	1	1	2	2							2
Contracts Managers	4	–	4	1			1		1	1	5
Site Agents	8	2	10	2	(1)	2			1		12
Senior General Foremen	4	–	4	–	(2)						4
General Foremen	4		4		(4)	1		1			6
Foremen	8	–	8		(4)	1		1	1	1	12
Section Foremen	9	–	9	–	(4)			1	1	1	12
Chargehands	N/A		N/A								N/A
Quantity Surveyors	4	2	6			2	1	1			7
Engineers	9		9	4		2	2	2	1	1	12
Senior Estimators	1		1			1					1
Estimator	1		1								1
Prod'n Planning Engr	–		1								1
Group Secretary	1		1								1
Accountant	1		1								1

Chargehands, skilled men and labour omitted. Note: arrows indicate promotions within the company

Table 7.5 Extract covering part of a manufacturing unit affected by product and technology change

Category	Actual Jan 1978	Movement 1978 Out Was	Out Red	Out Trs	In Trs	In Fop	In Rec	Plan Jan 1979	Movement 1979 Out Was	Out Red	Out Trs	In Trs	In Fop	In Rec	Plan Jan 1980	Movement 1980 Out Was	Out Red	Out Trs
AMP Dept																		
Semi-skilled 2	6		2					4			4							
Semi-skilled 1	48	4	18					25	2	2	22							
Skilled 2	36	4	14		2			20	2	8	10							
Skilled 1	10		4					6		6								
Highly skilled	4		2					2		2								
TOTAL	104	8	40		2			57	4	18	36				Nil			
BRLE Dept																		
Unskilled	9			3				6			6							
Semi-skilled 2	9			3				6			6							
Highly skilled	87	3	27					57		51	6							
TOTAL	105	3	27	6				69		51	18				Nil			
ETC																		
JPB Dept																		
Semi-skilled 2		20			60	10	60	110	80			150	10	95	265	100		
Semi-skilled 1		10			30	10	30	60	40			70	10	90	190	50		
Skilled 2		1			11	7	2	19	12			25	15	1	49	5		
Skilled 1					2			2	3			5	5	3	12	3		
TOTAL	Nil	31			103	27	92	191	135			250	30	179	515	158		

KEY: Was - wastage; Red - redundant; Trs - transfer; Fop - from other plants; Rec - recruit

The rundown of research staff offset by the build up of product
development staff will need to be detailed as the new jobs available
may not be attractive to the research people becoming available.
The longest possible period of 'early warning' is desirable in such
cases to enable the redeployment options to be investigated fully.

Table 7.4 was used by a civil engineering company to
summarise its needs over a five-year period. The opportunities for
promotions within the site management structure were seen to be
important, and as a result of the plan, much greater attention was
generated for the identification of people who might be promoted
and to their subsequent training and development.

Yet curiously little attention was focused on the engineers in
the company – possibly because the bulk of the business was in
sub-contracting on major contracts where the engineering work
was done already, and possibly because the company top
management was a mix of accountants and 'practical men'. As a
consultant in this situation, two of my key recommendations
were the strengthening of the engineering resource and a review
of the engineering input to company objectives.

Table 7.5 covers part of a manufacturing unit affected by
substantial product and technology changes. It includes areas in
rapid decline and other areas about to be launched. Significant
within the plan is identification of the fact that many skilled men
on existing products would be unlikely to accept the job
opportunities on the new lines which were largely semi-skilled
assembly in nature, so that an active recruitment and training
programme would be implemented during a parallel programme
of redundancy.

For brevity, only two of the departments planned to disappear
are shown, plus a summary of the group of departments in the new
area. These are sufficient to show the form of analysis, and the
types of movement expected to take place. Further, all supervision
and all service departments are excluded from the extract.

In general, the bulk of the lower skilled employees no longer
required in the 'old' areas can be offered equivalent graded jobs in
the new organisation, although a proportion, estimated at between
10 and 20 per cent in different areas after analysis of individual
cases, may prefer to take a redundancy package or early retirement.
In the early stages, the run down will be out of phase with the timing
of new requirements and some redundancies will arise for that reason.
(In reviewing the plan, some rescheduling of work was arranged to
bridge the gap, reduce redundancy needs and increase opportunity
for transfers.)

In the skilled areas, particularly the highly skilled group, there
was very little scope for absorbing those employees except into
lower grade positions. In view of the apparent national shortage

of highly skilled men, this was discouraged and in addition to generous severance terms, every assistance was given in obtaining alternative employment. A few rather narrowly specialised categories faced some difficulty in this respect. Many other skilled people ultimately expressed a preference for taking the redundancy package rather than the alternative jobs, which were at the same grade and pay levels although involving different work.

This case is a classic example of a change in skills-mix requirements, where assumptions about need for redundancy and scope for retraining and redeployment may be wildly out, due to the generosity of many redundancy packages. Continual review of actual events against plan is essential and it is likely that a plan such as in Table 7.5 will have some updating on a quarterly basis — in fact, there is an expanded version of this plan giving quarter-by-quarter figures.

Concealed within these figures can be skill mismatches where the grading of the two skills is identical, but there is no possibility of interchange between the employees concerned. For that reason, the use of 'skill-grading' as used in this case is not ideal, and should be sub-divided where relevant into distinct skill categories.

Figure 7.2 shows in a suitably disguised form, a summary of senior management requirements across a group of building companies (although it could be in any industry). It reveals a picture of needs with very little evidence of people ready to take over, and was, in fact, a first statement of management needs prepared in the group. Subsequently, they developed plans along the lines of those set out in Chapter 9, but at least once each year the board continued to review a 'current analysis' in this simple form to reassure themselves that some action was in hand to cover all management likely to move within about three years.

Additions to later lists were managers whose performance fell short of requirements and those rated as of high potential for early advancement.

Figure 7.3 is out of line with the rest in this group. The analysis followed a conclusion that the company had an increased need for industrial engineering effort, but that the existing total headcount in industrial engineering departments was too high.

The examples illustrate part of the problem: an ageing population of low (job) graded and poorly qualified people. The task of building an efficient, technically up-to-date department from this starting point could only be achieved over an extended time period, or by rather brutal surgery, for the existing situation had been permitted to continue up to this point with no real effort to modernise from previous planning studies.

A 'surgical' approach was proposed: a theoretical target structure was developed in full 'everyman' detail; short lists were developed for every post in the new structure from existing stock; where the new

To the Board   C O N F I D E N T I A L

SENIOR MANAGEMENT REQUIREMENTS AT 1978

*The top slice of a manpower plan becomes personalised. The
number of jobs tends not to change, but there is some change
in job contents and incumbents.*

South East

1 *The appointment of an MD to replace LMT on his promotion
   is required now. Shortlist attached.*
2 *Chief Buyer E.C.Able reaches retirement age of 62 on
   7 December 1980.*
3 *Chief Contracts Manager J.C.Beeson is 62 on 1 December
   1983.*
4 *Senior Contracts Manager T.D.Connock is 49 but suffers
   ill health and will need to be transferred and replaced.*
5 *Finance Manager A.H.Dennis is 31 and is unlikely to be in
   the same job beyond 1981.*

Central

1 *Chief Buyer G.R.Easy is over retirement age, and is 65
   this year.*
2 *Chief Contracts Manager G.G.Fredericks (38) is likely to
   have justified promotion by 1981.*
3 *A Branch Manager for the Western areas may be required
   by 1980.*

South West

1 *Joint Managing Director H.B.Griffiths is 60 in July 1979
   and wishes to retire at that date. The other Joint MD
   B.S.Herbert (46) will become sole MD.*
2 *Chief Contracts Manager S.P.Tilley (37) may be promoted
   before 1980.*
3 *Finance Manager S.B.Jacobs (29) is unlikely to be in the
   same job in 1981.*

Midlands

1 *An Md for the region has been selected and will be
   appointed shortly.*
2 *The present MD H.P.Kennedy is 62 in January 1978.*
3 *Finance Manager A.Litton could be a region MD within
   two years.*
4 *Chief Contracts Manager L.W.Mitchell is 59. He will be
   succeeded by F.N.Oswald.*
5 *Etc., etc.*

Figure 7.2 Extract from a senior management requirement
plan prepared as at 1 December 1977

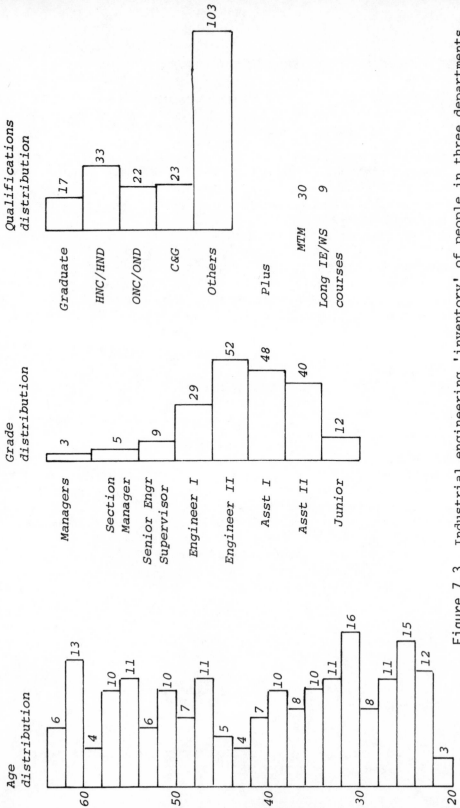

Figure 7.3   Industrial engineering 'inventory' of people in three departments

specifications could be met internally, existing people were appointed,
plus some compromise appointments on a probationary basis to
minimise the upheaval. Some 80 per cent of posts were filled internally, while external recruitment was necessary for the rest.

The remainder of the existing force was redeployed to other
work as far as practicable, but there were many casualties and an
uncomfortable industrial relations situation.

The lesson of this example is that quality is an important facet
of manning. If you need to upgrade quality it will require careful
and deliberate planning over several years in advance of the need.
Individuals can rarely change dramatically.

Had this company taken three years to implement the change,
it could have been done by working down from the top, ensuring
correct job specifications and calibre of people in the management
levels in the first year and definition of the supporting structure.
The second year would have enabled the middle structure to be
implemented, with slower-pace redeployment of unsuitable staff
and steady fall out of individuals who realised the form of the
change taking place and the fact that they did not fit. Intake of
higher calibre people into the bottom levels would also have been
a significant second-year development. The programme would
have been completed in the third year with a final comb out of
old guard, unsuitable people, and the new-styled structure should
have become fully effective.

A summary of these examples would be difficult as they
illustrate such a diversity of problems and approaches. I hope
they provide suggestions which help your own individual needs.
Common to most of them are the two factors I started with:

1   A clear picture of forward manpower requirements, in
     'exploded' form, to show detail by function, category and
     level at a specific or a series of points in time.
2   A clear picture of our current manpower inventory, also in
     'exploded' form using the same breakdown by function,
     category and level and to which we have applied the knowledge
     we have of the ways in which existing manpower is developing,
     being promoted, or leaving. This should also be summarised at
     the same points in time.

These tell us what we have to do with our existing manpower and
in terms of additional recruits to meet the specific manpower
requirements we have identified.

7.2   Planning action on excess manpower stock

During the initial comparison of forecast inventories against planned
requirements, we shall have identified many pockets of manpower

who at first sight will be excess to requirements. This section is concerned with the range of options open to deal with them.

First of all, we want to continue to employ all or most of them if this is practicable. They know the company and have expertise, much of which we may prefer not to lose. Certainly they have advantages over possible new employees who would have to get used to the company from scratch. So we are likely to examine seriously the possibilities of retraining and redeployment and only consider redundancy as an expensive last resort — though sometimes unavoidable.

Retraining and redeployment

Redeployment — employment of existing manpower on alternative work — may be possible without retraining, but usually some form of preparation for new work will be necessary.

Straightforward redeployment opportunities occur when a different part of the organisation has an immediate need for exactly the skills which are becoming available. Within a large group, central co-ordination of all vacancies at times of cutback may delay the filling of some positions marginally, but enables all available internal candidates to be given first consideration — which can be very important if there is a threat of possible redundancy.

A more normal situation is that the people being released are from jobs that cease to exist due to product or technology change and there is no prospect of identical work within the organisation. Then we need a breakdown of the skills used in the old jobs for comparison with analyses of skills required in other jobs for which there is an on-going demand. The objective is to match the skills or skill types as closely as possible, to establish job opportunities for which retraining is a practical and acceptable course.

Skills analysis is covered in some detail in the books on the subject by Douglas Seymour.

For example, one company found a close match between the skills used by fitters and toolmakers, whose work was in decline, and the requirements for other specialists such as some categories of computer programmer. They took an experimental batch and put them through an intensive two-week 'conversion course' which identified that rather more than half would be fully able to cope with the more extended retraining course, and allowed the others to drop back into their old jobs. In this way, they could reduce the manning levels in the declining areas on a controlled basis and provide a supply of good trainable material feeding into the new technology area. The enthusiasm of the people making the conversion was a major factor in the success of the programme,

although none had previously considered careers in the areas to
which they transferred.

It was the careful use of skills analysis which opened up this
retraining avenue. Significantly, it was not an expected or 'natural'
career route and the secret was, undoubtedly, an open-minded,
experimenting approach which paid off handsomely.

Another example is less dramatic, but socially significant. The
company was running down its heavier mechanical work and
developing far more light engineering sub-assembly work. The former
was traditionally men's work; the latter, women's work. Offered the
alternatives of redundancy, or similarly graded and paid sub-assembly
work, numbers of men began to accept the traditionally female jobs,
and after some initial unease expressed by both sexes, quickly
settled to competent performance.

Much other retraining involves updating or adapting existing skills
to new ideas or technological advance. While individuals have a
responsibility to themselves for keeping up to date, this is not always
possible, and the company input must be to create the environment
and the opportunity to keep knowledge and experience up with the
developing needs of the company.

There is one further option to consider under this heading. It is
possible, as an extreme measure in order to avoid redundancy in
some situations, to find a means of utilising people who are not ideal.
This may involve restructuring some jobs to a non-ideal form to
enable work to be done by non-ideal people, e.g. partial deskilling
of a job to enable lesser skilled people to be employed. While this
may be workable, it has to be recognised that it may have industrial
relations implications and even prove more expensive, and cannot
be recommended as a normal action. However, I have seen this
approach used to overcome a skill shortage, with full co-operation
of the skilled trade union involved.

Redundancy

To enforce redundancy is the last resort when there is no scope for
making reasonable and acceptable use of the employee.

Redundancy should not be considered socially unacceptable. It
will, almost invariably, be uncomfortable, both for the employee
made redundant and the manager responsible for handling him.
However, many employees look back on their redundancy with a
certain sense of relief. They could, for example, have been retained
in lower grades and less satisfying jobs, and become very dissatisfied.
A decision to make them redundant jolted them out of complacent
acceptance and resulted in an aggressive and successful search for a
job fully in line with their abilities, which they now enjoy.

I once had the misfortune to have to counsel a man whose original job had disappeared; who, out of 'compassion' had been retained in the company without a proper job. Although guaranteed 'security', he had suffered a nervous breakdown, despairing of having a worthwhile role in future. We agreed a basis for parting company and got down jointly to the task of seeking a new job outside the group. The immediate impact was a restoration of self-respect and, remarkably soon, a suitable external appointment.

From that time, I have not been frightened by redundancy situations. Two things are essential, though: fair — even generous — financial treatment of those who must be affected, with the option to volunteer if there can be any choice, and secondly, absolute maximum help in seeking out, applying for and hopefully getting other job offers. This direct assistance through to the point of taking up new appointments is an essential part of the releasing company's manpower policy and practice.

Taking terms first, these vary too much for generalisation here about amounts, except to suggest that national legislation is unlikely to be sufficient. Beyond this, the basis of the 'package' will probably need to be influenced by company requirements. If extended notice is being given (and the longest reasonable warning should be given), bonus payments for staying on until the company's requirements are met should be considered, in order to guarantee the required work force and plan the required rundown phasings. In other situations, bonuses may be paid to encourage immediate or speedy departure, but these situations should be rare for they indicate inadequate planning.

Some redundancies will be enforced because a plant is closing down, but other redundancies arise from a cutback in manpower levels and leave a degree of choice open to employees. In these situations, encouragement of volunteers can reduce or even remove the pressure. The opportunity to retire early on pension, or to collect a sizable sum sufficient to launch a small business; these can be highly attractive to some employees. In practice you may find an excess of volunteers and a need to be selective about who you release.

The need for careful counselling is as important among this group of volunteers as with enforced leavers. We need to be sure that volunteers are absolutely clear about their intentions and subsequent rights. Advice on the problems of a new small business should not be excluded from the 'service'.

For enforced redundancies, and particularly plant closures, generous and sympathetic guidance and help is essential. (I am picking up the story after the industrial negotiation which will have covered the closure.) The objective is to open the way to alternate work opportunities. We need to advise our people on

local work opportunities, or lack of them, together with other 163
options. We need to open an employment office on our premises,
and get other company recruiting staff to use that facility. We
may need to provide guidance on alternative careers, on retraining
opportunities, including adult training and other full-time courses.
We need guidance on being interviewed for long-service people.
In summary, we need to provide a full range of personal services
for the people affected, run, if the numbers are significant, by a
project manager committed solely to that task.

7.3   Training and development

The growth rate of an organisation is likely to be limited more by
its personnel than by any other factor. (Product marketability and
finance are relatively more purchasable commodities than personnel.)
The ability to maintain and hold good people is tied partially to
proper payment, but is influenced to an even greater extent by the
ability of a company to provide opportunities to each individual
to develop fully, to utilise his abilities to the full, and to find
continuing job satisfaction. (Few companies would neglect an
opportunity to improve an expensive machine in order to raise its
productivity or the quality of its output.)

Training and development plans are implementation plans which
follow identification of what we need to do, and the main part of
any training and development programme is directed towards
preparing individuals to meet future needs. The real objective of
company training and development programmes should be to help
optimise the use of the manpower resources of the enterprise, in
line with the needs of the enterprise. That means bringing as closely
into parallel as possible, the abilities, ambitions and interests of
employees, with the people requirements of the business. It means
that developing people in any aspect of manufacturing is outside
the requirement of a purely distribution and service organisation,
and should not be undertaken, however 'suitable' the people (unless
the company is planning a radical change of activity).

The first requirement is a clear picture of the training and
development contribution that can be made by the company on
existing manpower and planned intake to be most effective in the
jobs they perform now — and as planned for the future. Determination of this requirement will have involved analysis of the manpower
requirement plans against existing manpower inventory and forecast
changes in the content and abilities of the inventory; and from this,
the training needs of all employees and particularly those expected
to grow or to change their jobs over the plan period. Further, we
shall assess likely training needs of expected new intake.

If a type of trained staff is not readily available, or only available by poaching people from other companies, it becomes necessary for an employer to set up his own production line. This will be a training course which has a throughput of the forecast requirements in the categories concerned.

The most clear-cut example of this sort is the apprentice training scheme. The majority of these cover a five-year period of training and provide an essential supply of skilled workers. The intake, after allowing for wastage, must relate to the anticipated requirements at the end of the training period.

However, a great deal of training is of very much shorter duration, and the problems that arise are related to the difficulty of extracting a man in a job from his work commitments for the period concerned. These training sessions are still primarily designed to develop skills and abilities specifically required by the company, but the secondary function of training is to enable an individual to develop his innate abilities to the full extent of his increasing capacity for absorbing and comprehending new knowledge.

Next, the method of providing the relevant training or development, and the creation of the right environment to encourage learning will be identified. We need to know how various categories of people best learn various types of subjects, or acquire information. We shall design training courses to meet these requirements most effectively and economically in terms of time as well as financial terms.

Finally, we shall need some form of audit to ensure that the objectives of the various parts of our training and development programme really are being fulfilled. This audit will include feedback arrangements to ensure that we as programme managers learn continually about the effectiveness of the things we do, to back up the principles of efficiency and economy in our training and development effort.

Training is a very expensive activity. To put a number on it, some major companies have made detailed analyses of their annual training expenditure, and come up with figures around 4 per cent of annual payroll cost. While something approaching 90 per cent of this is in the costs of wages, salaries and overheads of the people actually being trained, with something around 10-12 per cent on the analysis and development of training packages, and the costs of training space, equipment and trainers, the figures are large by any standards. For this level of expenditure, companies generally want to see clear training objectives which can be monitored afterwards. As one company put it, the only measure of success is that the employee can do the job for which he is being trained to a high level of ability within the shortest possible time. Certainly, we must talk of 'cost effective' training.

A company of some 20,000 people had a very good training

department of 18, but was doing badly in its main business. The board of the company agreed that some of their training packages could be marketed and before long, the 18-man training department was generating more profit than the 20,000 man business.

There is an approach to training which says that the most important factor is the avoidance of training levy (or maximising training grant); that training is carried out with that objective and any other benefits are incidental. This approach is clearly evident in a number of companies.

The direct financial impact of training activity arising from the training levy and grant system cannot be ignored. It demands an administration system to record everything done. The important thing is to make sure the right things are done. To find out what these are, a periodic assessment of training needs is essential.

Training needs assessment

A fully comprehensive assessment of the training needs across a company is a major task, but it will ensure that training objectives can be established with precision for a two to three year period. The basics of this assessment fall into the following parts:

1   Training needs of individuals in their present jobs, as identified by performance appraisal, and including updating of knowhow.
2   Training needs of individuals in preparation for possible future jobs, as identified by assessment of potential abilities and succession planning.
3   Training needs to meet changing company requirements, identified centrally rather than individually. These would cover changing policies and procedures, or response to changing technology, such as requirements for new skills. They would cover both existing employees and the preparation of additional people to meet changing company needs.
4   Training schemes of a longer-term nature to take in groups of people to meet future requirements. For example, apprentice training schemes produce skilled men after five years, so that the intake rate needs to parallel the expected requirements at that future point. Graduate intake schemes have a similar long-term infeed to lower level management positions.

Data against these headings will provide a sound basis for determining the training objectives of the company, and point to the facilities required. The decisions regarding facilities will, in turn, determine the time required to meet the various parts of the overall programme.

From experience, the full requirements identified tend to require the maximum resources likely to be allocated for up to five years (during which time, new requirements will arise). The objectives have to take this into account, and evolve a commercially realistic training programme, taking into account a management assessment of priorities.

It is important to note at this point, that in the course of a typical year, the training people may take up to 5 per cent of an employee's time — usually less; that his manager will be involved for the other 95 per cent of the year. An important part of every training programme is to make sure that each manager carries out the maximum possible amount of training and developing of his subordinates as possible.

An extract from a typical analysis of training needs is shown in Figure 7.4. Down the left-hand side is a breakdown of functions or skills. I have seen a company-wide analysis on sheets where the listing covered some 200 headings, so choose the extent of your breakdown with care. Across the top is the level of training required, on which I will enlarge briefly:

1 *General*   This covers the level of knowledge necessary to enable a manager to supervise/direct the activity, without being or becoming a specialist.
2 *Familiarisation*   This covers the subject in sufficient depth to enable the 'trainee' to work with a specialist in the subject; for example, with systems and programming specialists where the work of the 'trainee's' department is to be prepared for computerisation; or with basic accounting where a technical man is to become more involved in budgeting or costing.
3 *Detail — advanced*   This is for the 'doer' in the subject, to advance his detailed knowledge of his subject. Most training would cover specific and generally narrow segments.
4 *Detail — basic*   Training in the subject for staff engaged in that field, or broadening into it.

For the training needs analysis to be meaningful, it is essential that the individual appraisals of performance and assessments of potential should be as realistic and accurate as possible. This calls for competence in skills analysis on the part of each manager, at least in respect of the positions reporting to him, and also on the part of the personnel or training staff involved in both appraisal and the preparation of the training needs analysis. (It is also essential for anyone involved in any form of job restructuring.)

Consider for a moment the job of a design engineer, and the skills required for effective performance — which are more extensive than is immediately evident from the title. The job includes:

1 A requirement for certain basic technical knowledge.
2 A creative element, a skill or ability to apply the technical

Function or skill	General	Familiarisation	Detail	
			Advanced	Basic
1 Man management				

Managing people
Motivating and
  leading
Training and
  development
Salary and wage
  administration
IR
Participative
  skills, etc.				

2 Finance				
Financial man- *agement* *Cost accounting* *Budgeting, etc.*				
3 Marketing and selling				
Industrial selling, *etc.*				
4 Manufacturing				

Manufacturing
  management
Planning and
  scheduling
Purchasing, etc.				

5				
6				
7				
Etc.				

Figure 7.4 Training needs analysis schedule (format)

knowledge to meet a stated requirement, or a new situation.

3   Cost awareness; a knowledge of alternative materials and their qualities and costs.

4   An understanding of how things are made, so that his designs can be manufactured within equipment and cost limits.

5   An understanding of selling and customer requirements which can temper his design inclinations. Also an ability to 'sell' his ideas.

6   Reasonable personal relationships with his manager; with his equals; with subordinates. This probably includes an ability to communicate well.

Most middle to senior jobs have a similarly wide range of skill requirements, which must be well balanced for effective performance of the job and which are identified informally, at least. Examination of this design engineer list provides pointers to the general context of these lists; knowhow related directly to the job; more general knowledge about other functions; and aspects of 'people' skills.

It is sufficient here to draw attention to skills analysis, and the role it plays in establishing training needs assessments — and, ultimately, training programmes. At the same time, it provides indications of whether 'trainees' will tend to be naturally successful in learning new skills, by enabling simple comparison between skills they have acquired and new skills proposed — a valuable guide where retraining and redeployment are involved.

Training forms

Training (and development) activities take on a variety of forms. Training may be near full-time, largely internal, such as apprentice training, teaching basic skills, or a mix of internal and external, teaching a vast range of personal or technical skills, either in depth or at a surface level. Let us look quickly at some of the main areas:

Basic skills training   Under this heading are included those forms of near-to-full-time formal training and sandwich courses which are effectively an extension of full-time education, yet against a different background and with more specific purpose. While the industrial and commercial flavour influences the content of the scheme, the value of the training is initially much greater for the individual than for the employer, who anticipates a long-term return on investment.

This assures that the employer will subsequently ensure adequate salary and career advance to hold the employee, who is not otherwise tied to him. Basic skills training can be an expensive waste for an employer, or it can provide an exceedingly valuable nucleus of employees who have a deeper than usual appreciation of the company.

Apprenticeships for junior employees, either in manual skills or in commercial and office activities, make up the greater part of basic skills training volume. This training is essentially continued education, combined with induction to industry or commerce. It answers a continuous need for employees competent in a range of basic activities required by the company.

Advanced technical training for the next strata of employees, to assist them to obtain formal qualifications, represents the 'A' stream of basic training. It ensures the same type of supply, in this case of technical people with practical experience, into the 'junior officer' grades of the organisation.

Management skills training   Under this heading come all the types of training designed to draw out latent supervisory skills, and those other abilities or qualities necessary for the effective direction of the work of others. Whether or not those skills are 'built-in' to an individual, the act of supervising is rarely totally understood before experience, but training can draw attention to the essential actions and the form the responsibility may take, so that the fledgling supervisor is prepared for what follows.

Supervisory training of newly appointed staff, and also of established supervisors in additional aspects of their work, constitutes a major proportion of the activity under this heading. Course subjects and length are extremely varied and it is impossible to generalise. Some organisations concentrate on newly appointed men, putting new chargehands and foremen, or office supervisors, through up to a month of full-time training. Other organisations prefer one- to three-day sessions on specific topics, held as frequently as possible.

Work supervisors appreciate short, case-study type sessions on problems of industrial relations, based on their own official procedures, so that they are briefed on how to react to shop-floor problems. The office supervisor is more concerned with changes in staff structure, counselling procedures and in case studies on salary administration.

Basically, supervisory training is concerned with the handling of problems which the less experienced supervisor might find difficult. Guidance on providing leadership and comparable activities runs as a theme behind the specific course subjects.

Graduate trainees are a rather special category of future managers. Their training is generally more a matter of induction to industry than specific training in management. During this induction, they are likely to spend periods on ordinary supervisory and other formal training, while the bulk of their time is applied to seeing and doing as great a variety of work as the training supervisor has been able to

arrange. This type of training — the development of experience — is
the subject of the next main section.

Management training is a phase with such wide-ranging implications
that it is difficult to know where to begin. Forced to a definition,
one would talk of basic education in man management — the
organisation, integration, direction and leadership of a team; and in
the use of various modern management tools and thinking.

Of the training form, one would think of the type of course
attended by groups of developing managers of similar potential.
They assemble to discuss case studies and to participate in guided
discussion groups, business games and the like. One might also recall
the comparable arrangements for very senior and established
executives set on a higher plane; and the tutorial type of individually
tailored training that is proving highly effective.

Specialist skills   Almost as an extension of the management
training paragraphs above, but applicable to staff at every level,
comes training in specialist skills to enable an individual from a
specialised role towards broader responsibilities, or to enable the
line manager to appreciate a special subject in greater depth. Such
courses are an important part of development training.

There is a multitude of these specialist courses, covering almost
any subject one could imagine and going on continuously. They
cater for all levels of knowledge and competence, so that the
required course for a particular individual is likely to be found if
sought.

The specialist production engineer about to be appointed to a
management post might benefit from certain finance and perhaps
man-management courses, as a preliminary and in addition to any
training in straightforward skills. The older chief cost accountant
becoming finance manager may appreciate a three-day refresher spell
on the latest management accounting methods. The specialist staff
recruiting officer may gain an appreciation of several other aspects
of personnel work from a series of one-day to one-week courses.
Irrespective of whether courses are run inside or outside a company,
the planned contact with new or different ideas pays off.

A secondary but highly important aspect of this type of training
is in the opportunities it provides for meeting similarly employed
people and discussing ways common problems have been tackled.
In fact, sessions planned to draw out open discussion of problems,
rather than devoted to a series of talks, are often the most appreciated
and useful.

Formal training provides information and ideas, whether in one's
own field or in new territory, and gives an appreciation of theory.
What it cannot do, beyond quite narrow limits, is to provide
operational know-how, which leads us into the next section.

The purpose of development assignments is to provide operational experience, expand confidence and generally prepare the recipient for greater responsibility. They provide a balance to the injections of primarily theoretical knowledge, which come from formal training.

John Smith starts his career as graduate entrant and management trainee, and finishes as managing director. The path he may have taken on the way has been the subject of a number of studies. His career may have unfolded within one company, or he may have been forced to move about in order to achieve his promotional steps.

While most individuals are interested in advancing their own careers, managers and supervisors also have a responsibility for advancing the careers of their staff. If this is to be done successfully, the development requirements of each individual must be appraised and his career assignments planned accordingly.

When considering individual development, one tends to be influenced by the existing 'normal' pattern of career paths, although it does not follow that these should be accepted as universally valid. In this country, the general pattern has been for individuals to work their way up within a job family stream. Thus, it would be rare to find a top production post being filled by a man with a largely marketing background; and not common to find a sales manager moving into a market research post.

This degree of specialisation, running from top to bottom, is inhibiting, yet provides a challenge to development planning. As any plan must look ahead, the employee who is expected to become marketing director must be provided with the broadest possible pattern of experience covering the various facets of marketing, yet must progress up the career ladder as he does so. A large part of the purpose of development is to fill in the experience gaps, and to overcome any weak points. It is vital that good people, capable of moving into wider spheres of responsibility, should be given opportunities to move into new areas and broaden their experience. This is most easily done through the medium of a series of steps through associated posts.

Development assignments are generally designed to provide a specific type of experience which an individual is considered to need. For example, if he is to go into a post with a large supervisory content, an interim assignment leading a small project group or heading a small team may be valuable to him. From this, he gets the feel of directing, guiding, leading, encouraging and counselling people who are responsible to him, and is then prepared to cope with a much larger group.

A second form of development assignment is the sideways move to a different function. The recruitment supervisor put in charge of an industrial relations unit may be temporarily out of his depth on technical experience, but uses his personality to take effective control of the team to support himself and to learn from them.

At a more extreme level, the accountant placed in charge of a technical administration department must come to terms with technical staff and learn to understand their jargon. By doing so, he proves able to hold a post with a wider span of activity extending over non-financial functions.

An exceptional case might be the younger man selected as potential director material, and possibly managing director material. Early experience in the general management of a small unit, preceded by responsibilities in more than one function, provides a start. Subsequent periods in senior roles in each of the prime functions of the business, at progressive levels if this is possible, and tending to administration rather than highly technical roles, prepare the ground for his overall responsibility. Most of us will know of actual cases that followed this pattern.

Development planning

A development plan will generally be based on the needs of the organisation, and will be designed to provide candidates for all those 'boxes' likely to be vacant over the next few years. Each of the boxes will be duly marked with the names of possible incumbents. The development operation will be designed to prepare those individuals for the anticipated vacancy, and the potential candidate who lacks certain types of experience must be assisted.

> In the highly technical, engineering department of an electronics division, the impending retirement of the chief engineer meant that his chosen replacement, a senior research engineer, had to be broadened. This was done by some outside specialist training and through two assignments. One of these was a 'special duties' assignment – drawing up the plan for a five-year development programme for a new project – and was essentially administrative; the second was to launch the programme, directing a series of project units and preparing a successor to take over. In the two and a half years he spent on this work, he broadened from a back-room scientist to a planner and leader.

In this case, his latent abilities had already been seen and recognised, and his technical ability was unchallenged. He himself recognised his need to broaden, and accepted personal development without being aware of the further assignment and appointment being considered for him.

The main point to notice about development in line with known
requirements is that there is little to be gained, and many disadvant-
ages, in developing people haphazardly according to their own and
their managers' whims. The preparation of a company's better people
for non-existent vacancies can only encourage their departure to
other organisations, so that vacancies that do arise must be filled
from outside.

Job rotation

The development of the scientist to replace a retiring chief engineer,
in the example above, is a typical instance of job rotation in a
development setting. The classic case occurs in the introduction of
graduate staff to various activities of the company. By spending
significant periods in a series of posts, a young man with high
potential acquires a sound basic knowledge of first-level company
operations.

Alternatively, this rotation may be within one function. Three
years spent holding first-level posts in recruitment, training,
industrial relations, job analysis, general personnel work at shop-
floor level, or others, provide a very sound basis for building a
specialist personnel career. At more senior levels, the plan is more
individual, tending to be designed to fit a particular individual.

In a mass production process factory (a division of a major
company) the promotion of the general manager was planned
in 18 months' time. In turn the production manager would
be promoted to general manager. Although a member of the
factory executive committee, the production man was
admittedly weak on financial matters.

He was given an appointment as assistant division controller
in one of the large divisions of the group, a post aside from
the line control, but involving him in the financial management
without direct day-to-day pressure. For five months he set his
own work programme, guided loosely by the comptroller,
learning the intricacies of operations and planning. After some
some ten months, he returned to his own division in a curious
position of joint division comptroller until appointment as
general manager. (The more logical title of assistant general
manager was rejected in accord with a wish to keep the general
manager's move secret, but the unusual nature of the interim
appointment caused hardly less speculation.)

Job rotation is planned to fit circumstances. Designed to prepare
one individual primarily for one particular post, plans are tailored
to fit on a one-off basis. The common factors are the questions to be
answered as a guide:

1   What additional experience does Mr X need in order to do job
         'B' competently?'
     2   What specific assignments or appointments would give him
         this experience without affecting the company's operations?

Assignments and appointments

Assignments and appointments aside from the main stream of career
advance tend to be relatively short term, and general use of normal
supervisor or manager roles is not acceptable if interference with day-
to-day running may become excessive.

Within a large organisation, certain posts tend to become, or may
be deliberately labelled as, developed positions, although a selection
of other posts are also used. The posts normally used for development will be a little out of the main firing line, without tight dead-
lines on their operations, inclined to be concerned with administration,
planning or analysis. These same functions typify the special assignments which may be given, often embodied in a temporary appointment as 'assistant, with special responsibilities for reviewing X, Y and Z'.

A particular form of development appointment, used for groups
of young potential managers a few years ago, was the creation of
'junior boards'. These were generally looked upon as informal sub-
committees associated with executive committees, and assigned
specific tasks on which they had to take action. Introduced to the
atmosphere of executive committee working, and faced with the
fact that they were influencing a significant aspect of the
organisation's work, the members were spurred to think and act on
broader lines than any to which they had previously been accustomed.

This idea has not gained very wide use, possibly because of
difficulties in collecting a suitable and balanced group, and also of
selecting suitable projects. I suppose the substitute is the playing of
'business games', where the participants may be selected from one
or a variety of companies to 'work' in an imaginary business. A
computer is used, programmed with a 'business environment', and
the group's actions are processed by the computer against the
environment. The 'game' can be as stimulating intellectually, and as
sobering, as the real thing.

The majority, but not all, development assignments will prove
successful. Detailed analysis of achievements during an assignment,
especially where these can take place against the background of set
targets, provide the facility for extracting maximum benefit from
the project. A series of open discussion sessions enables every aspect
of requirement and action to be reviewed, and other ways of handling
situations examined. From this concluding phase, the man may learn
as much again about the role he has played temporarily.

'I never teach my pupils. I only attempt to create an environment in which they can learn.'

'I like to learn, but I hate to be taught.'

These two comments illustrate perfectly the task of the training manager. More than anything else, he must create the right environment and stimulate interest in learning. After all, the learning process is going on all the time. Much of our ordinary living teaches us something more each day about people and about the things we are doing, but the extent to which we learn by these experiences varies greatly and it is up to us what we get out of them. A good training manager stimulates the desire to gain more from experiences and creates situations in which the relevant experiences occur. To do this, he needs to know our training requirements, their relevant priorities and our preferences.

Training breaks down when the real training needs are not being tackled, and where the form of training is 'teaching' and creates resistance. In a permissive era when, from five years old, children are given the option of involvement in lessons or doing something else, it is hardly surprising that most adults resist 'teaching'. A training man can lecture for fifteen minutes to introduce a subject. After that, he needs open discussion to retain interest, or leave the groups to work at a project or case study carefully designed to enable the 'trainees' to draw appropriate conclusions. The role of the training man is not 'schoolmaster', but rather creator of learning experiences, and perhaps 'ringmaster' in discussion groups.

The personal relationship between the tutor and trainee (at any level) is important, and needs to be one of mutually accepted equality in an industrial training situation. If that is lacking and antagonism towards the trainer develops, his ability to get any useful message across becomes non-existant.

A further requirement of the training environment is some form of feedback on learning. I recall an incident in a building construction company, where non-technical trainees running a management training programme used practical case study material to show how planning could speed up the process of high-rise building. Lack of conviction on the part of early participants that the 'theory-boys' had valid points to make was overcome when they put the concept into practice on return to their units. Subsequent training sessions were much more acceptable, partly because the material used and competence of the trainers was proven, but also because the 'trainees' had feedback in terms of proving to themselves that they could apply the new ideas in practical situations.

This brief section assumes that we started our training and development programmes from clear objectives — from clearly identified and defined training needs. Further, that the programmes implemented were those designed to meet those needs. From that starting point, we have a sound basis for assessing what we achieved — except for several fringe factors. For example, most training takes a long time to 'mature' and is difficult to quantify anyway.

Much training and development is designed to modify and improve behaviour or practice in the job. However, the immediate managers of all our training will have comparable objectives, and they have the 'trainees' for at least 95 per cent of the year compared with relatively small periods of time spent on most training.

Precise evaluation of effectiveness is near impossible, and we are reduced to a series of judgements, and seeking out specific examples of 'undiluted' training impact: for example, the success of an across-the-board training programme to introduce some new concept into company practice. Even here, other 'political' type factors may produce side effects, and the assessments made endeavour to identify and separate these.

I approach this enigmatic question cautiously, with questions of my own. For example, 'Is the training programme sufficient?' — or 'Are these training needs not tackled?' 'Do we have sufficient resources?' While this does not review *quality*, it does review one key factor. If the answer should be clearly that not enough training action is taking place to enable us to meet known requirements of 'trainee' output, the company training programme is falling short of objectives.

But is the quality of techniques good enough? More than one training programme has been more-than-adequately resourced numerically and financially, but has lacked something in the calibre of its training people so that the end results have been ineffective. I'm not preaching for the latest jargon and techniques. Far from it. But there is a definite need for comprehension of what can be achieved, and how, and an ability to make it all hang together and work. By no means all 'training people' have this flow.

A useful measure is the supply of potential supervisors internally. There may be other factors such as financial motivation to contend with, but if you are not generating an adequate supply of would-be supervisors through your training programmes, once again, you are falling short on what should be a key objective.

Finally, there is no harm in asking whether your training programme is making any real contribution to company performance. Try and show specifically and positively that it is. Apart from stimulating the intellect, it will show you whether you can talk the right language with the people in your company who should be

approving your training budget. If you can't convince them it is all
worth while, revert to square one and look again at your objectives.

7.4   Planning recruitment action

All recruitment action, indeed all action of any sort that leads to the
appointment of an individual to do any job, requires the completion
of a sequence of logical steps:

1   The organisation in which the job is located must be clearly
     defined and approved.
2   The individual job to be filled must be clearly defined and
     approved.
3   The need for the job to be filled at the present time and into
     the immediate future (at least one year) must be clearly
     accepted.
4   The inclusion of the job in current or flexed budgets, or some
     properly approved addition, must be clearly identified.
5   There must be visible effort to fill the post from internal
     sources.
6   In the event of no internal candidates being suitable, we should
     know whether the external market is likely to yield the 'package'
     of experience and skills we seek, from local or national market
     surveys.
7   External recruitment action, and selection.

   In the remainder of this section, I shall go quickly through the
relevant aspects of these steps.

Establish the vacancy — steps 1, 2 and 3

As each vacancy arises, a procedure must operate designed to appoint
the best available man, while utilising the opportunity to progress an
existing employee.

   'Jones is leaving. Replace him!' or, 'Get me another man for
design work'.

   Simple enough instructions admittedly, but why is Jones leaving?
Could it be that the organisation is changing imperceptibly and that
the change in work, unnoticed by a poor supervisor, has unsettled
Jones?

   Throw in one doubt of this sort and it becomes worth checking
carefully on the real vacancy before steps are taken to fill it. If the
post is a new one, its requirements and duties need to be adequately
defined.

   The review of the job is best done by interview with the job holder,
where one exists, or with the immediate supervisor. If a job description

exists as a starting point, the review should set out to determine if and how it has changed. However, lack of an earlier job description is not critical, as it need not take long to obtain a complete outline of the post.

More important at this stage is an evaluation of the particular problems that the new man will have to face and the qualities he will require. For example, a marketing man may have to be prepared to cope with rapidly growing and undefined new competition; a personnel man may have to create a special retraining programme to prepare for impending automation of the plant.

Once the job content is confirmed, the job grade can be checked and a recruiting salary range determined. Within a normal grading structure, the overall salary range will be immediately available, but occasionally some special range may apply to a particular market group, so a quick check on values should be automatic. Additionally, the precise type of individual required will influence the commencing level, e.g. minimum experience to meet specification at the minimum salary, or a special rate to take account of potentially useful extras.

Establish the vacancy — step 4

However clearly the job is established and the urgent need made evident, *it should not be possible* to proceed with filling the post until it is equally clearly established that the position has been budgeted for, and the expense is expected. At any time, a variety of smooth-tongued managers can justify recruiting additional people, but if these were not taken into consideration in business plans and budgets, what will be the impact of their actions on the total picture? It takes little enough time to set out a brief supplementary plan to justify unbudgeted action and show the expected impact, and is an essential discipline in manpower control.

Is the position budgeted, or covered by a flexing of the budget, or covered by an approved supplementary plan?

And if it is, take a final confirmatory look at the requirement, and ensure the position is for essential work or an important discretionary role: for work which must be carried out as part of the basic business operation, or work which is not essential, but which is being carried out at managements' discretion, freshly restated.

Internal sourcing — step 5

Once the vacancy is clearly established and approved, we can consider sourcing.

Outside recruitment of any sort is expensive so that, apart from all the other reasons, the need to examine and make use of the 'existing stock' makes economic sense. The search within the company can take one of two main approaches. It can leave the initiative to the individual, after letting him know what vacancies exist; or it can make use of all available information on staff and endeavour to match the job requirement, and at the same time progress an individual's career.

Taking the former case first, this approach may overlook the best candidates who may not apply for a variety of reasons. These may vary from simple lack of adequate understanding of the vacant post or underrating their own abilities, to straightforward pressure from a selfish supervisor. However, in recent years, more managements have overcome their inhibitions, and have made much more information about vacancies and salaries available to staff.

Even if the company adopts the second approach, there is no reason why internal advertising should not be continued in moderation, as a cross-check on the basic approach, however effective this may be, and as an escape valve for employees who want to let off steam.

Internal advertising also serves a useful purpose in drawing attention to potential transfer and promotion prospects within the organisation, and emphasising an intention to develop staff from within rather then replace from outside. Further advantage comes from identifying staff who are unsettled, or who are known to want to move for any reason. These people are potential leavers whom you may retain by taking action of some sort. At least you will have been warned!

Where a company assumes the whole responsibility for internal selection, it must ensure that it has the facilities to identify all employees potentially able to fill a vacancy, and can select the best choice with a minimum of employee participation. If it adopts this course, it must ensure that it obtains adequate publicity for its procedure, which must be visibly effective. The personnel department acquires a knowledge of staff potential which, combined with data on experience and performance, provides a valuable guide to available and suitable talent within the organisation.

This general comment assumes that the vacant position has not been anticipated, possibly arising from a termination. Where the vacancy is known in advance, planning to fill it may be possible as the situation may be looked on at leisure as a potential career step for an individual, and the possibilities of training up or otherwise preparing the selected employee in advance of appointment are considerable. Not least in importance is the feasibility of sitting alongside the previous job holder for a period, in order to pick up the reins at first hand.

Not all internal placements will necessarily be ideal. Occasionally, the only man with sufficient experience or knowledge must be appointed for particular reasons when the vacancy is unexpected. On these rare occasions, the possibility of revising the job content should be considered in order to reduce any adverse effect of a possibly poor choice. Such a situation might arise in a technical department, where the available 'deputy' is a brilliant specialist who is hopeless at administration. The department might be restructured to consist of a small, high-powered specialist group with a good administrative officer, plus a separate 'services' department containing the bulk of personnel and operating in parallel. The first opportunity to reunite the two groups should obviously be taken.

This last example leads on to a further aspect of internal selection – that of finding a job for the man, rather than the man for the job. Most organisations have their square pegs. Many are established employees with many good qualities – people the company does not want to lose, but who have lost ground in a changing organisation.

A list of square pegs probably rests on the majority of selection officers' desks, and the search for suitable places for them is constant. These places may be anywhere. Chain movement may help to solve a problem, and at the same time develop an individual and fill a vacancy. The first stage must be to identify the special requirements in a possible job, in terms of man and job specifications, grade level, working relationships and so on. From this first point, it should be possible to isolate areas within which to keep a watch.

External sourcing – the market – step 6

Assessment of the market supply situation is essential, as not all our future requirements can be met from existing stock, and the skills we require may not be freely available on the market. If we should need to recruit people to train ourselves, we must have sufficient lead time.

Knowledge of the present and probable future of the market is essential to manpower supply planning. It is at this critical stage that a manpower plan may be aborted and a fresh approach demanded; for if the market is very tight and requirements cannot be met by recruitment, we need to consider alternatives which must include reconsideration of basic commercial objectives.

Knowledge of the availability of various categories of individuals or skills is therefore very important – together with assessments of the way these are likely to change.

The first part can be provided with some accuracy by most

recruitment staff as they acquire an excellent 'feel' of the market place. The second is more difficult.

To gain a reasonable picture of future supply, I have found it necessary to build up a picture of total supply and demand for the category concerned. This may involve finding out the industry or national growth in demand, and then assessing the total possible supply from all sources, and the probable loss rates to the industry — retirements, etc.

Where you need people who are in short supply, this is the only sure way of assessing the likelihood of being able to meet your own requirements.

In one study, the supply position showed that, at best, the manpower likely to be available in certain high skilled categories would be 70 per cent of the requirement in the industry in five years time. Also, the company's present turnover was 40 per cent a year in these categories, so they were unlikely to be able to retain a stable work force. Studies were begun immediately to evaluate ways in which the work could be restructured to make use of less skilled manpower in order to cope with volume.

In passing, consider the position of companies in the industry which were not forewarned!

Returning in more detail to assessments of the present market, reports are compiled most easily by recruitment staff as they are in closest touch with the manpower market and with local DoE statistics, but many other people may add some intelligence report to the picture. For example, news of redundancy in another company may indicate that categories of staff normally in short supply are temporarily available.

The analysis needs to be as specific as possible on when, where, calibre, price, and so on. For example, people may be available from another industry but need retraining before becoming effective. The type and length of training required must be known if the data are to be usable. An entry on the list might read:

Cost accounting   Staff with ACWA in short supply and require supervisory posts; no high-calibre specialists available locally. Staff with intermediate CWA available from company 'A' from time to time — mainly failures from their training scheme. Unqualified but experienced costing staff freely available.

Also valuable is a list of categories that are virtually unobtainable, and data on possible supply sources, or contacts. As these special categories must be recruited from time to time, the more information collected in this way, the more likelihood there is of obtaining a suitable candidate. However, these lists also indicate those groups of employees we should be at special pains not to lose, and whom to the greatest possible extent we should underpin by other staff under training. And if we are likely to need many additional people in these categories, the case for launching an adequate training programme is very strong.

This brings me back to the national level, for severe shortages are often widespread. Effective manpower planning at a national level should gradually reduce the occurrence of situations of this sort. At present, once a shortage has occurred, only a 'crash' training programme can ease the situation if the demand does not slacken.

External sourcing — recruitment — step 7

Once the decision is taken, and the job clearly defined, the recruitment process can follow. The basic process is too well known and too well covered by authoritative writing to need coverage here. The old NIIP publication, *The Seven-Point Plan,* is recommended basic reading. Use of consultants; advertisements under box numbers rather than use of the company's name; where to advertise; what detail to give — all these are outside the scope of this book.

Planning recruitment involves detailed short-term planning and the process involves scheduling the recruitment of the various staff required, taking into account any time necessary to define the post, prepare and publish any advertisement, sort and interview candidates, select the most able and perhaps negotiate terms, and then wait while notice is worked before he joins. The times will vary for a number of reasons, such as the ease or difficulty of attracting suitable candidates, and the differing lengths of notice required. The result is that, with varying periods of induction to allow for, initiation of a recruitment campaign may need to begin anything from three weeks to a year before an individual is required to become effective.

Recruitment from external sources may be into training schemes planned to develop individuals to fill specific groups of jobs, or direct entry to vacant posts.

Direct entry recruitment at senior levels is sometimes looked on as reflecting badly on a management development scheme. Yet it must be clear that some specialist posts must normally be filled from nationally small numbers of suitable people, and that 'fresh blood' from outside to fill an unexpected senior vacancy may be healthy from time to time. The succession plan that sets out to fill every vacancy from within may tend to become excessively inward-looking, thus leading to some narrowing in the evolution of the company's thinking.

External selection, then, serves a dual purpose. Apart from filling a particular vacancy, it provides an opportunity to inject a shot of different thinking. Of course, the injection should not be too revolutionary, and the 'package' should fit reasonably with the

company's existing staff (no long-haired and green-corduroyed
economists for City merchant bankers!).

Conclusion

Effective selection and placement will be achieved by progressing
each vacancy through a series of stages:
1   Establish that the vacancy exists officially and confirm the
     real requirement.
2   Evaluate all sources of supply of the staff required, particularly
     internal sources.
3   Review the available individuals and select for future, as well
     as immediate, employment.

MANPOWER CONTROL AND AUDIT

Planning provides the basis for control. If we think our way systematically through all the options open to us and come to a defined set of conclusions in the form of plans for action, it would be totally illogical to stop there, rather than go on to monitor our actual progress against the plans. That monitoring covers every facet of the plan, starting with the basic assumptions around which the plan is built, for if these change, the whole plan must be 'flexed' around the revised assumptions.

If we assume that our sales volume will be 100,000 units and subsequently orders enable us to aim for 115,000, the manpower requirements will be affected, materials intake will be affected, and the whole plan flexed around the changed needs. Usually, a range of assumptions will change in various ways and the formal plan is only the starting point for flexing.

Further, we require a steady feedback on much of the detail in the plan. For example, we need data on the actual manpower situation, including costs, against the standards built into the plan. If the plan calls for reductions in manpower which are not being achieved, the excess costs of overmanning may imply a serious threat to the unit's ability to meet its profit objectives. This review, or audit, is a basis for controlling our progress against the plan and brings reality into what could become a theoretical study rather than a practical business plan.

The studies and plan identify a problem and means of overcoming it, but somehow this lacks reality to a 'down-to-earth' management unused to dealing with problems they cannot touch. Their control system avoids the annoyance of constant reminders and nothing happens until the problem strikes home. Then action is too small and too late.

Planning provides an Early Warning System. If you don't intend
to act when warned, don't waste money on planning.

All company controls should have their roots in plans. All
company plans should have a follow through check on achievement.
All controls should be flexible in relation to changes in the basic
assumptions on which the plan is built up.

8.1 Manpower controls

Manpower control is concerned with achieving agreed manning
standards across the organisation:
1   As built into plans and budgets.
2   Subsequently flexed for changes in assumptions.
3   Subsequently improved by better utilisation, or changed systems,
     etc.
This sounds simple, but we have seen the difficulties and comp-
lexities of establishing manning standards, and know by experience
the constant fluctuation in work volumes and content, available
manpower, and short-term forecasts. The manpower 'controller'
must constantly balance out all the pressures within the business
and aim to achieve the best use of manpower. The critical single
objective is to optimise utilisation — to achieve the best possible
productivity — for the many small changes within the business are
much quicker acting than his ability to adjust his manning levels,
either up or down.

A control is required on all manpower movements if any form
of manpower control is to be effective. It is not enough to control
recruitment while leaving no control on internal transfers for this
could permit manpower to build up to excessive levels from internal
movement. Every single appointment made must be subject to the
control procedure.

The procedure required will ensure that the position is properly
authorised in every way before being filled. Even in small companies,
the philosophy should be identical, even if the administrative
routines are simplified to the point of the managing director asking
a few questions. We need to know that the position properly exists
in a defined organisation; that the job is clearly defined, together
with man specification; that it has been built into the current
budget, or flexed budget if sales or product mix have been changed;
or that there is a clear supplementary budget. (We might add here a
need to watch the incoming order position very closely, particularly
in fast changing markets where order positions have been known to
dry up suddenly leaving manpower requirements radically changed.)

These establish a 'legitimate' request. I believe that there are
further requirements. Although proper manning standards have been

used to establish the budgeted requirement, and no subsequent change in standards has occurred, is the standard still valid? Is there any alternative way of getting the work done? Indeed, is all the work of the department still essential? I hold the view that investigation of the real need is an important step in approving the filling of every vacancy. Only when it is clearly established that the post must be filled should authority to fill it be given.

This may sound an extended ritual, wrapped up in red tape – and no doubt it could be. However, it can be reduced to a straight-forward and automatic discipline that takes very little time, and causes delay only when the thinking has lacked clarity and saves unnecessary appointments being made.

A useful routine in a larger company would require a series of signatures on pre-appointment documents, simply confirming that the line managers concerned have ensured that specified checks have been completed, and including the local managing director and his head of manning standards. I would ensure that a proportion of these were carefully audited.

Why make every case a subject for fresh review? Firstly, because the detailed work of almost every department changes slowly, and the 'incident' of a position being filled is opportunity to see whether manning standards should be updated or not. Most checks will go through very quickly, but a sufficient proportion throw up changes for automatic review to be fully justified. Without it, I would suggest that unnecessary manpower, equivalent to 5 per cent of the total, could be absorbed into the organisation annually. Look around you at some of the results.

In this process of reviewing requirements, I believe that some of the best controls exist where management of a company or division has pushed the real control on manning standards and use of man-power back down to the supervisors, and at the same time encouraged them to make use of the basic data already at their fingertips to watch their manpower productivity.

A supervisor, given a moderate degree of guidance, can establish these factors of loading which influence his manpower requirements. The supervisor of a small pool typing invoices will know how many invoices a day one of her girls can manage, as a normal rate. If the input rises and stays at a higher level, additional typing resources will be required. If the volume falls, the resource need falls.

The pool supervisor can see, on a daily basis, how many invoices have been typed by each girl (adjusted for absence, etc.) and also see the intray and backlog positions. She may seek ways of increasing the average throughput per typist and spreading the load over peaks and troughs of volume, in order to optimise the use of her staff.

This is a simple example, but it explains the basic approach. If a supervisor is involved in this way in determining how best to use his manpower and in determining at what points some change in the level of manning is necessary, and most of all, if his decisions and judgements are accepted, he becomes personally committed to manning standards generally tighter than any which might be imposed.

One factor for the supervisor to consider is the size of his backlog of work at any stage. If the workload is variable, his manning should be such that at the lowest work intake phases, his backlog approches or just reaches nil, but ideally never reaches the point where work runs out and people are idle. In an unplanned situation, periods of idle time in such a department are considered normal, but by accepting a backlog of work at peak intake times and phasing work through to other periods, utilisation of people is improved, a larger volume of work is covered by each person, and there has been no increase in pace.

'Backlog control' is an excellent technique for supervisors in departments with workloads that vary, but follow some pattern. It gives the supervisor a simple basis for observing his day-to-day manpower utilisation, and he more than anyone else sees the result of too many people during the trough periods. He is the individual most motivated to get his manning into line with needs over the whole period, and he knows he is well armed with data to prove the need for additional manpower if there is an upswing in volume.

The objective of manpower control operation should be to operate at this supervisory level. Management confidence builds up on the evidence of supervisor-controlled weekly graphs of manpower utilisation, showing patterns of achieved improvements.

Control on requisitions for manpower must cover every manpower movement; all appointments, internal and external, including all transfers and all recruitment; all temporary or agency employees; even all job and grade changes. After all, a grade change can mean a 10 to 20 per cent increase in pay levels for people affected!

Manning standards should include statements of the grade levels, for in the end, the objective of a manpower control system is cost control. The remuneration and benefit costs may total up to 30, 40, or even 50 per cent of the value of sales, and it is control of this massive expenditure which really concerns us.

Who should control manpower? The short and obvious answer is the chief executive, but in a large organisation, the responsibility has to be delegated. In theory, the logical direction for delegation is to personnel as the function dealing with manpower. Sometimes this will work, but a conflict of interests is likely to develop. The personnel function has responsibilities for employees and their welfare, and for industrial relations negotiations. Close awareness and involvement in the business itself, and the manpower requirement is, curiously, seen as a conflicting interest and some personnel departments are not geared to manage an effective manpower planning and control function.

The alternatives of placing the responsibility with industrial engineering or with systems are not acceptable to me. I believe it is important to link the function closely with personnel in most organisations, and to make sure that the personnel staff are commercially involved rather than commercially naive.

8.2   Manpower audit

Physical control against standards and plans really needs a further activity for 'How do we know that the system has been working as we planned, and that our plans have been properly implemented?'

We need feedback on what has actually happened, and we need to audit how it happened.

Our regular headcount summaries should tell us whether our overhead manpower trend is in line with our forecast from approval of manpower requisitions, and hopefully, the analysis will show breakdowns of actual manpower against flexed budgets for companies, divisions and departments. Anything seriously wrong would be evident from this analysis.

What else do we need? Let us look at some of the possibilities.

Audit of requisition control   With all the care that goes into manpower requisition control, how many appointments slip through the net, and in what circumstances. The audit should check through a selected batch of personnel records and identify the requisition approval of each recorded change. This may reveal that some categories of transfer tend not to be covered by approvals and indicate a major hole in the control system.

A second check would be of departmental records of who is employed and what they do, against personnel or payroll records. On occasion, there are differences, because local management just do things in order to get round paperwork. A favourite form of 'correction' is to amend the salary review sheets with all the implemented but unofficial changes.

The third check is for agency or temporary employees, padding out the manning levels without proper approvals or recognised needs. I know of a division that uncovered Bill and Ben — two agency employees who had come in thirteen years earlier, and were never recognised as part of the headcount until a detailed audit was carried out. Almost all audits of the use of temporary and contract staff lead to immediate savings.

Audit of manning against manning standards   When manning standards are revised, it may be appropriate to leave a few existing people in position who are identified as excess to the new standards. Over a period of a few months, natural wastage and transfers will remove the problem and questions of redundancy of forced transfers are avoided.

Unfortunately, a few managers and supervisors are exceptionally able at maintaining their over-strength establishments, somehow managing to get replacements even when someone does transfer or leave. It is these cases that the audit seeks to identify. There may be a need to confirm that the standards are correct, but then positive effort must be made to get the actual manning into line with standards, and to keep the department or the manager 'red-circled' for close control in future. All manpower controllers get to know the empire builders quickly.

Where a major cut-back of requirement is being played at low key, it may be appropriate to give up to a year for actual manning to drop to the new level without enforced wastage. However, we should expect to see some progress towards the new levels and should audit at least quarterly for evidence of intent.

Audit of manpower utilisation   At any one time, there are a number of manpower categories in short supply, either locally or nationally, but impacting on the operation of the company. An audit is necessary to examine how well we use our existing employees in the skill categories concerned.

I assume that all the obvious things within the present structure and systems have been done, and that utilisation looks – on the surface – to be good. The audit should take the form of a special study, to see whether some fundamental change, such as re-structuring of work, is achievable, for such a move may completely relieve the current shortage for the company. I have been involved in successful restructuring work in response to shortage of occupations as diverse as computer systems and programming staff, welders and development engineers.

Although the pressure to improve utilisation is particularly strong at times of shortage, audits of utilisation should be encouraged wherever there is a 'feel' that standards fall short of what might be achievable, or where employees are leaving the company because they feel they are underemployed.

Audit of manning systems   Where any system has been in use for a number of years, examine it to ensure that it is providing all that is required, and that there is no provision of unnecessary or unused statistics, tabulations, reports, or forms of any sort.

The requirements from manning systems evolve continuously. The regular attention of a systems man is essential, as much to ensure that some activities are discontinued or reduced in frequency, as to enable fresh demands to be met.

Audit of the manpower control system is especially important on a continuing basis, particularly following changes of key personnel as new people may misinterpret procedures or modify rules. Similarly, audit of procedures for establishing manning standards are important. For example, are the routines for following up on a systems change or capital expenditure, justified on grounds of expected manpower savings, being followed through promptly so that revised standards are built into plans and controls, and implemented?

Slippage in potential manning standards, due to sloppy administration and lack of audit, is one of the major loopholes in manpower control. In fact, control can become a ridiculous joke, if all the surface procedures are followed, involving significant expense and use of analysts, but the finishing touches are omitted from the system. The concept of a 'field analyst' in a large company, constantly out in the subsidiaries and divisions to audit requisition control and manning standards is a good one. It is a job for a high calibre analyst and excellent for broadening appreciation of the total, detailed operation of the organisation, probably changing hands at around two-year intervals.

Audit of recruitment, training and development actions One of the most critical features of manpower planning programmes has been in the way that recognised needs for advanced recruitment or for specific training and development programmes have been defined but not implemented. I find it astonishing that this should happen as frequently as it does, with drifting inaction building up much more serious needs by the time a further annual plan is assembled.

Senior managers today are very busy people. They have to determine their priorities and allocate time to the most important issues, delegating less important work — but checking to see it is done. Too often, the implementation stages of manpower planning get lost in this maze, without recognition of the potential impact on the business, and are undersold by the manpower planners. It is rarely enough to accept 'full agreement' from a senior manager as absolute assurance that action will follow. Persistant follow-up to ensure action is initiated, properly resourced and effective is necessary.

The audit requirement arises at least quarterly, simply to ensure that the implementation plans are being implemented and the objectives met. If they are not being met, it becomes necessary to 'flag' that important assumptions about manpower supply are ceasing to be correct.

As one example, if it is assumed in the business plan that fifty additional development engineering staff will be recruited in a difficult market by mid-year to support a key programme and, at the end of the first quarter, no major recruitment programme is running, then it is evident that the new team is very unlikely to be ready in time and the development programme will be delayed. Delays in important training programmes can have equivalent impacts.

Other audits   This list cannot be complete for every organisation. For example, have manning budgets been 'flexed' for changes in sales and production volumes mix before controls are applied? Each company must identify its own special requirements and establish the means for carrying out the audits.

Chapter Nine

MANPOWER PLANNING FOR MANAGERIAL POSITIONS

9.1   Introduction

Above a certain level manpower planning ceases to be a matter of numbers by category, and becomes linked to individual positions and individual encumbants. There will probably be some numbers in the overall company planning covering these senior levels, but we can really forget the numbers and concentrate on the fine detail. The group of individuals we are likely to be dealing with in this way will rarely exceed a couple of hundred, and it will be well within the ability of one individual to be involved in, and fully aware of, the entire plan in detail; however, the plan must not be over-simplified and should contain all the following activities:

1   Definition of the overall objectives for the company plus those for significant units, plus the associated purposed-designed organisation structures: *(a)* now, *(b)* at points in the future.
2   Definition of individual management jobs, their objectives in major difficulties foreseen, their inter-relationships including staff and line man specifications: *(a)* now, *(b)* at points of change in the future.
3   Definitions of limitations imposed by the development of individual people, intellectual, psychological, personality, probable rate of development, skill, flexibility, mobility, acceptability, individual preferences.
4   Definition of development requirements and actions for all individuals within the plan.
5   Statistical probabilities of individuals leaving the organisation or of death.

   From these activities and analyses we can build up, first, a plan

in theory, then develop a plan around people for operation and
finally establish a basis for auditing progress.

The measure of success is that the company should always be effectively organised and managed.

People are a company's most important assets. But the company is rarely free to develop its employees at maximum pace in the direction ideally suited to their individual capabilities. The compromise to be achieved is that the company's requirements should be matched as closely as possible, or even adapted, in order to provide optimum scope for the developing potential of its employees.

What I choose to call career planning here might be better recognised under titles such as 'management development' or 'succession planning', or even 'manpower planning', but I mean something more than these titles generally imply. The philosophy of development does not stop short at management, and the purpose is not simply to nominate successors. The real questions which should concern us are:

1   Are we making the best use of the talent we have, and have we an adequate provision for future management requirements?
2   Are our employees satisfied with their growth in terms of advancing their careers?

The present and future manpower needs of the company have been analysed as part of the planning described in the preceding chapters, and inventories of current staff indicate the present position. The identification of individuals to fill planned future posts enables us to ensure that they may be suitably prepared in advance, and that they will be properly employed continuously. But what staff feel about their present job and possible future assignments has a very direct bearing on the situation, as we shall see. In fact, we should consider the employee's viewpoint and try to understand it before we look at the company's planning and development operations to fill its management situation.

9.2   The employee's viewpoint

What is the employee looking for, or expecting from his employer, beyond the basic reward of salary and benefit? Job satisfaction and credit for achievements certainly stand very high on his list. Inevitably he is also much concerned with opportunity for job scope to expand in parallel with growth in his work capacity. Linked to this, there may be motivation in the form of a positive demand for complementary salary growth, or some form of desire for 'power', a need for intellectual challenge growth to maintain job satisfaction, or a combination of several factors. Recently we have seen increased

recognition of needs for wider interests, for more independant home
life and social activities. Often, the individual may be largely unaware
of the reason behind his driving force.

Sublimation of ambition may be possible for a limited time and
to a limited degree, without damage. But once the drive is side-
tracked into gardening or being treasurer of the local wine-making
society, or being a shop steward, the prospect of regaining the former
career drive appears to be substantially reduced.

For both the employee and employer this means either consistent
work achievement and satisfactory development within an organisation,
or movement outside in search of either the right job opportunity, or
some other form of transfer of interests. The man of high calibre, and
with his sights set high, is unlikely to accept any work situation in
which he feels he may not grow satisfactorily. The effect of his
loss on the company's growth potential is unlikely to interest him;
his loyalty (if that is the right word) will be held only by prospect
of advancement. Whether his post is at the top, middle, or lower
levels of the organisation will make little or no difference to his
outlook.

The employee assessing his own future prospects is likely to look
for a number of general pointers to the company's attitude, for
signs of scope to develop, and for indications of potential hazards.
He will look for:
1   Signs of effective staff planning and development.
2   Signs of an interest in his own case.
3   Apparent scope for advancement (as opposed to blocked paths).
4   The possibility that jobs of particular interest may become
     available.
5   The existence of 'personality' problems.

By taking a close look at these five, we may obtain a much greater
understanding of what an employer needs to do and show.

1   Signs of effective staff planning and development   An individual
thinking about his own future looks round the organisation and
assesses which jobs he would like to do. He notices staff movement;
do staff leave in frustration or not? If they are moved around, does
the movement appear to be planned to satisfy individual development,
or merely haphazard? Is the changeover as people retire smooth and
planned, or last-minute action? From his personal analysis and
discussions with his colleagues, he will judge whether the management and the personnel staff are competent people to participate
with him in the development of his own career.

2   Signs of interest in his own case   The obvious sign to the
employee of the company's awareness and interest is a career move
to broaden his experience, or a promotion, but actual movement

rarely takes place at intervals much shorter than two years, and the period is usually longer. Much more significant and more frequent are the performance and career discussions with his supervisor or manager. The employee with his eye on his future appreciates these part-casual and part-formal discussions perhaps two or three times a year. However, it is one thing to carry out these discussions, but quite another to make them effective and satisfying. The employee is talking about his career; a subject on which he is highly sensitive. He is going to look for genuine interest from his manager, for an appreciation of his value and potential, and real intention to ensure his career progression. Words without intention become obvious soon enough, and lost confidence and trust in the company take a long time to re-build.

3   Apparent scope for advancement   A company, or department, with a large proportion of staff in any one age group has a serious built-in problem for any young man looking ahead. An ageing management group can sometimes mean a blinkered and frustrating outlook, unless it is old enough to be near retiring age with the prospect of a number of imminent vacancies.

The feeling that there is a queue waiting for any vacancy is oppressive. The young man with talent but short service may be justified in moving out, and may only be retained if he is sure of his prospects of moving.

In a growth company, the employees who can see new posts appearing steadily, and going to outstanding suitable employees, is likely to feel confident that his own efforts will pay off. Should the appointments be rather more haphazard with too many going to outside recruits, the growth element is unlikely to prove so attractive.

4   Jobs of particular interest   Many specialists tend to mark out 'plum' operational jobs which they are convinced they could do. The prospect of a good move to a line post, or to a different advisory post providing broadening, is attractive. The specialist thinking this way may look round at people with similar backgrounds to his own, seeking for evidence that the right sort of movement does take place.

The less specialised individual casts his eye over the whole range of existing and possible posts in his own general field. Probably he appraises the people who 'stand in his way', who occupy or may be in line for the more coveted positions. Undoubtedly, he assesses his chances of attaining one in the face of the opposition, but he may look even more closely at the degree of mobility previously shown by the present incumbents, and is as much concerned by excessive mobility as by stagnation, preferring evidence of planned and progressive movement.

5 *Personality problems*   In any organisation, it is essential for an executive to be able to get on with those he must work with and for, and with those who will work for him. Unfortunately, there are times when two personalities do clash and so action to separate them is necessary. These incidents should not result in 'black marks' against the managers concerned (unless they happen continually to one individual) for part of the strength of an organisation is in the drive and personality of its individual managers.

Many organisations attract to themselves certain types of employee. This may not be universally true, but the tough go-getter is more at home in an aggressive marketing organisation and out of place in a sleepy, easy-going establishment.

Selection procedures tend to weed out the non-acceptable and stream the 'socially approved' forward for short-listing ('socially approved' being related to the company's likes and dislikes). Even so, a proportion of the new blood in any company will tend to be 'outsiders'; non-typical candidates, rather than brilliant non-conformists.

The new employee in a fresh environment will have considered whether it was 'his sort' of company at the interview stages. On joining, he will set out to establish friendly relations with those he must work with, and if it turns out that he cannot achieve this, he is unlikely to be able to do his job properly, or expect to progress very far.

9.3   The company's viewpoint

As most organisations are in business with the primary objective of making a profit, what does a company expect to get out of career planning? Clearly, this is a time-consuming and thoughtful activity, so what is the return on effort? As vacancies would presumably continue to be filled as they occurred, with or without career planning, the justification lies elsewhere, and there are four points worth specific comment:

1   Recruitment is an expensive and time-consuming business, so anything that reduces turnover, especially of the better people, is economically sound. Apart from the very substantial costs of recruitment, there may be extended periods where a job is vacant or filled inadequately, during which time, the probabilities of bad errors or omissions must be serious. Career planning especially encourages the development and retention of good people, avoiding the loss of their knowledge to the company, and generally assuring continuity. It also facilitates the achievement of optimum manning standards as jobs and people change.

2   The planned preparation of an employee for a new role ensures that he is effective immediately and not from a date months later. In an important new assignment, timing can make the difference between success and failure, as delay enables competitors to react.

3   Job growth has to be recognised and accommodated. Time and time again, rapidly expanding businesses have misunderstood what was happening to the content of senior posts, and have arrived at situations where jobs have totally outgrown the people in them. This situation is always difficult, but appreciation gives time to prepare and manoeuvre acceptable or face-saving actions, or overcome the problem completely by training and development.

4   Finally, from time to time an employee is lost to the company unexpectedly and at short notice so that normal succession planning procedures may not be operative. If his position should be a key one then urgent action is required. Potential replacements for all key positions should have been identified. The individual selected may be being groomed for some other post, but considered as 'reserve' for the post in question. For each vacancy which will or may exist, not only does the company need to know who is most able to fill it, but also what further development and training he requires before he does so.

The man — his readiness for promotion

A man at work is gradually changing, extending his knowledge, his experience of a variety of situations, his physique, his motivation. These things affect most directly the way in which he carries out his present job, but they also influence his potential ability to carry out other jobs.

There are many ways in which companies appraise their staff and assess those who are potentially capable of taking on bigger jobs. Appraisal is one of the fundamental parts of career planning. The manager who says of one of his staff 'This man is ready for promotion to shipping supervisor', must be confident that the man could step into the post tomorrow and cope with it reasonably well.

Competition

In most situations, more than one individual will apply for a vacant post which would involve a promotion. Even if the post is not advertised and is quite unknown to staff, the question of selecting the new man (or woman) may be made difficult by an excess of talent. A review of other preferable uses of candidates may help to reduce the list.

At least one major organisation deliberately recruits an excess of lower and middle management personnel to ensure maximum competition within the company, and the widest possible range of people from which to select. With a no more than average proportion of promotion opportunities, it is inevitable that they lose some extremely good people who miss out only because of the quality of the competition. I doubt whether this practice really pays in the long run, unless the planned movement of the best people is extremely skilfully arranged.

Training requirements

As individuals develop over months and years, their experience may be in too narrow a field to make immediate promotion possible, except within their own specialist functions. Where this occurs, and the individuals have all the other attributes of a promotion prospect, the company may try to arrange some form of broadening experience as preparation for a move. Each plan would be related to the type of career movement foreseen for the individual concerned, as the development of people is very much an individual matter.

Regarding training needs, virtually any training requirement can be met from the very wide options of training courses available, or alternatively planning individual tuition under a retained tutor.

In any list of staff suitable for promotion to a particular post, some will be fully ready to step into it, while others will require further experience or training. Training is most expensive in terms of time, and needs to be tailored to the company's as well as the individual employee's requirements.

Manpower requirements

Lastly, under the company requirements, the company's knowledge of its future manpower requirements influences its whole attitude to career planning. To take a fairly extreme example, the company whose needs will be small owing to a general cut-back in its activities may deliberately minimise development of staff but even in such extreme situations, managerial competence is required to get the best out of a declining market.

Knowledge of the requirements sets the framework for the company's career planning operations, and it is to the form of these operations that we look next.

A career plan requires a total review of employees now and as they may be developed, against a background of the organisation now and as it is planned ahead, comparable with the approach to manpower planning generally. Such a planning exercise cannot, perhaps, be described as scientific. Certainly, the procedure is systematic, and there are decisions to be made, however inconclusive these may be in that they are constantly open to review up to the point of action. Perhaps career planning would be most accurately described as an art.

If we are to look at the broad picture of career planning, we need something more than notes and forms and summaries; we need a TOTAL picture. I repeat, from the beginning of this chapter, that the plan should contain all the following activities:

1   Definition of the overall objectives for the company plus those for significant units, plus the associated purpose-designed organisation structures: *(a)* now, *(b)* at points in the future.
2   Definition of individual management jobs, their objectives in major difficulties foreseen, their inter-relationships including staff and line man specifications: *(a)* now, *(b)* at points of change in the future.
3   Definitions of limitations imposed by the development of individual people, intellectual, psychological, personality, probable rate of development, skill, flexibility, mobility, acceptability, individual preferences.
4   Definition of development requirements and actions for all individuals within the plan.
5   Statistical probabilities of individuals leaving the organisation, or of death.

Presntation of this assembly of data in visual form, and its subsequent use in career planning, can best be shown by a series of examples. The first of these, Figure 9.1, shows in detail the way information for one post may be presented on an organisation sheet.

The planning charts

Figures 9.2-9.5 represents a sequence of actual planning charts, suitably disguised. These are in black and white, although the company (and most users) make use of colours. Symbols and shadings are used to represent colours in the examples shown.

The example series is set in a division of a major company, but might equally be in a smaller independent unit. The sales turnover is in the region of £10 million. The product, which needs continuous technical research in addition to development, is sold

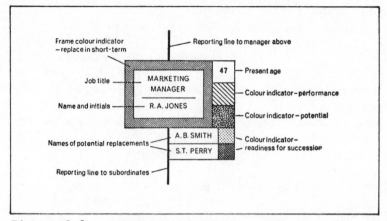

Figure 9.1 Detailed example covering one post from a career planning chart

through a network of some 30 technical salesmen in the United Kingdom and through a separate export agency to overseas markets.

At the beginning of the sequence, the 'old-stagers' are still running the company. However, the impact of the coming, younger regime is strongly felt in the planning, perhaps too strongly at one or two points, but reflecting an aggressive head-office or chairman's interest.

For simplicity, the charts reproduced cover only the two levels below the general manager, although in the example taken, subsidiary charts exist to cover all supervisory posts. These charts are prepared and held by the functional department managers.

The first chart, Figure 9.2, represents an audit of the present position. Each post is shown in relative order of value to the company, linked to the grade-level scale at the side. Against each post is shown the present job holder, his age in the current year, and an indication of his performance and potential, which is backed up by a set of reports. In addition, the names of potential successors are shown under the boxes, in all cases for the top line and, where especially relevant, for other posts.

On actual company charts, substantial use is made of colour to highlight certain of these points, and to bring out additional ones. For example, posts held by staff aged over 60 are surrounded by a red border to attract special attention. And the readiness of staff to take on a particular post for which they are shown as possible candidates is shown by coloured dots and symbols to provide a quick reference, and to differentiate between the immediate candidate and the longer-term prospect.

Before we analyse this chart, let us take a quick look at the content of Figures 9.3-9.5. Each shows the upper levels of the company organisation plan set out to show the distinct jobs and

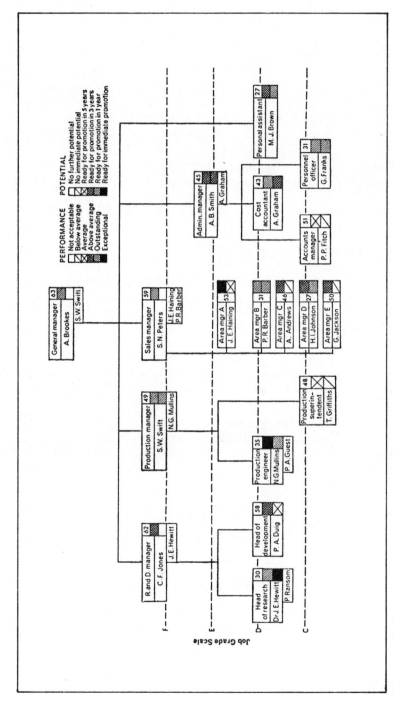

Figure 9.2 The present position – management audit

their relative levels at distinct points in time. No further appraisal
data is included, but the (often relevant) age is retained. In addition,
potential replacements are shown wherever possible. In the last of
the series, the lack of identified suitable candidates is highlighted
by the appearance of blanks and queries.

Analysis of Figure 9.2   Several of the senior posts are filled by
older men whose retirement during the period of the plan must be
faced. However, in most cases, a number of bright, younger men
exist ready to step up, so that the problem is not acute. In fact,
some deliberate development had taken place in the past with
this in mind. But the research and development group appears
rather poorly supported, the deadweight of older men having
tended to discourage the better men from the development side in
the past. We shall look closer at this problem on the development
plans.

   The bigger problem, not brought out on the present chart, is that
of anticipated growth. Movement to greater turnover and company
capacity, increased competitiveness and more sophistication in
management, will continue to raise the value of jobs in the near
future. This means that the growth in capacity of an employee may
be wholly absorbed by parallel growth in the size and complexity
of his present job.

   In fact it is this pressure which sets the problem, which is shown
most clearly by comparisons of job positions against the grade-level
scale at the side of each chart. Basic specifications for the functions
at each growth stage were sketched out in the organisation and
manpower planning exercises and support the grade changes. They
also set provisional 'man specifications' which help career planning.

   Completing the appraisal of the present position, we take a
preliminary look for problem areas. All top posts appear to be
adequately covered by potential replacements, although the
administration manager's cover looks thin in relation to future
growth. However, at the age of 45 in this company environment,
Mr. Smith is unlikely to leave or die, and the short-term risk is
acceptable.

The one-year plan – Figure 9.3   The changes scheduled for the
first year give an indication of further developments to come. A
gradual handover of the top post is to be arranged by Swift moving
up to deputy general manager and handing over his old post. We
expect Dr Hewitt to 'champ at the bit' at this stage as he waits his
turn to move up as well, and anticipate the possibility that a con-
cessionary title of 'deputy' may help. However, it need not be
charted.

   In the marketing function, evolution from straightforward selling

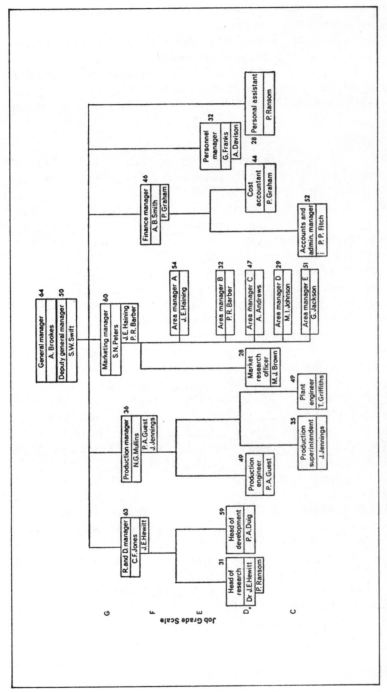

Figure 9.3 One-year forecast position

into a marketing organisation can begin. The present PA to the general manager's office is an economist who is being 'broadened' before his assignment to initiate market research and intelligence work. His place as PA will be taken by the young research scientist, Ransom, again for broadening until he becomes head of research.

Other scheduled changes include the change in job emphasis from accounting to finance, the passing down of routine administrative responsibilities, and the splitting away of an independent personnel activity.

The two-year plan – Figure 9.4   Mr Swift firmly in the top seat, Dr Hewitt appointed R & D Manager, and the average age in top posts down from the present 56 to 43 years.

The remaining senior executive in sight of retirement age, Peters, holding the key marketing responsibility, has no clear successor. The choice appears to be between the older Haining, only six years younger than the present occupant, and younger Barker, a man of high potential who may not have sufficient experience to cope with the big and growing post. Looking five to six years ahead, it may be preferable to appoint Haining as 'caretaker' for five years until Barker is ready, but this would not be an ideal arrangement.

So, in the two-year plan, the new post of sales manager is created as a preparation post for whichever one is to succeed Peters. During the intermediate two years, Barker will be given every encouragement to grow fast and, if he can stand the pace of growth, will step above Haining at that time. The critical decision cannot be delayed longer, and if serious doubt of both men still remains, an outside appointment will be made to ensure succession.

The potential weakness of the R&D organisation is also clearly revealed by this plan. Should Dr Hewitt or Ransom leave, there are no replacements available, and no successor exists to cover Mr Duig's sideways move. A deliberate recruitment effort is required to bring in suitable people over the coming two years, and an interim organisation of 'special' appointments may be necessary to attract good people without involving personality clashes.

Some shortage of potential area managers is also revealed, which the company hope will be overcome by a re-appraisal of their salesmen. As often happens, these outside employees have tended to be overlooked on formal appraisal exercises, and several are insufficiently known to their managers.

The five-year plan – Figure 9.5   In five years' time the organisation will be substantially different, and the size and complexity of the top jobs substantially greater. The plan shows the men most likely to be in the positions at that time. It is accepted, though, that this

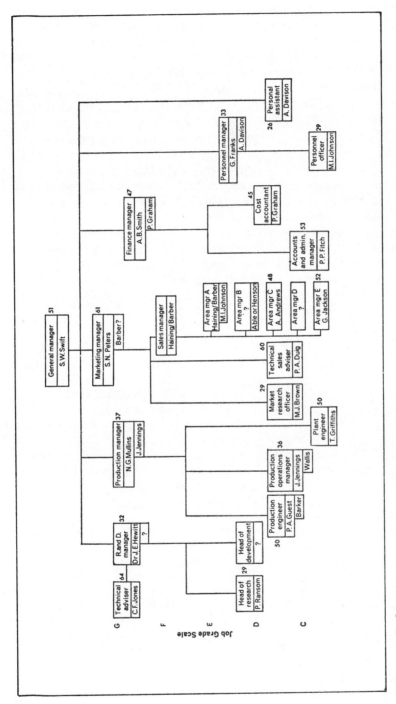

Figure 9.4 Two-year forecast position

selection will be regularly reviewed to ensure that each individual is growing at an appropriate rate.

Consider, as an example, the case of Mr Mullins. He is to be promoted from production engineer to production manager within the next year, at the age of 36. He must 'run-in' his successor as production engineer, get down to a much wider range of problems, get on top of the rapidly expanding production facilities and labour problems, and give thought to planning the second factory which is to be launched as a major project three years after he takes over. Mr Mullins is a qualified mechanical and production engineer who spent some time as a production chargehand and foreman before switching to production engineering and rising rapidly to the top. A well balanced individual, he wants to be production manager, so that in addition to the necessary ability and energy, he has the necessary determination to get on top of his job and control it. In every way, he fits the requirement.

Dr Hewitt, on the other hand, is less ideal. Heavily biased towards basic research, he is bored (at present) by such mundane things as commercial activities. Inclined to impulsive actions for some obscure 'principle', he may find difficulty in building up a product development activity, and in taking part in the upper reaches of management.

Should the charted plan begin to look seriously unsound, Dr Hewitt will need to be side-tracked as research manager, and a development manager appointed to take responsibility for the commercial exploitation of research. These alternatives to the main plan, generally alternatives which have been considered but rejected, must remain on the sidelines until a decision is irrevocably taken.

Concluding the discussion of this example series, which happens to show no interdivisional staff movement in the style of a small independent unit, I suggest that the approach and planning lines taken are typical, as far as any lines can be typical where no two situations are alike and the range of variation is enormous.

The static organisation

The company's basic problem in the example above was to obtain sufficient people of suitable calibre fast enough for their needs — the classic situation. Hence employees with potential at all levels must be identified and developed. The type and form of development depends on the future job and employee requirements.

In some other example, with limited or no company growth, and perhaps with an age distribution creating development blocks, scope for the development of individuals may be so severely inhibited

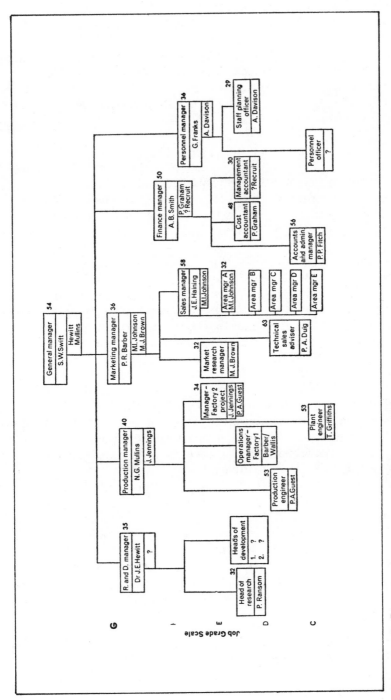

Figure 9.5 Five-year forecast position

that the loss of high-calibre staff must be accepted, simply because no alternative course of action is feasible. In such a situation the planner can only take a very long-term view.

To maintain morale as high as possible, turnover must be accepted to the point of assisting men to move when they wish. Also, poor performers must be side-tracked to facilitate maximum development of staff retained, and thus phased in with long-term personnel and business development.

Interdivisional development

The small- or medium-sized organisation can generally look at its complete career development plan at one time. The groups of companies, whether operating through a series of subsidiaries, divisions, or regions, will tend to have plans prepared in each major unit.

To ensure that the very best use is being made of all staff, it is necessary to bring these unit plans together for audit — for example, to ensure that the shortages highlighted by one unit cannot be met from a surplus elsewhere, and that the very bright young deputy accountant whose progress is blocked in division 'A' could not fit the imminent vacancy for an accountant in division 'B'.

It is especially at this group-wide stage that one encounters resistance to transfer, for there are still very many managers who cannot, or will not, see that they will lose the man whose career path is blocked anyway; whereas, by supporting internal movement, they will inevitably be on the receiving end from time to time. Even those managers who normally support career development theory may occasionally feel that 'it is a bit much' to transfer Jones 'just as he was beginning to be really useful'.

Faced with this argument, all one can do is to quote as much favourable case law as possible. Of course, it is hard on the unit or manager losing a good man, but get him to look at the other side of the picture. A reminder of the swift transfer to his staff of Mr Brown from division 'C', to replace one of his supervisors who left suddenly, may particularly help to emphasise the two-way nature of staff planning generally.

The 'high flier'

The young man of exceptional ability and drive invariably creates a career planning problem. His growth in ability and demand for greater scope may be so rapid that it is extremely difficult to see ahead for more than about a year. Even if a realistic assessment was made, scepticism would be too great for acceptance. To a degree, it becomes necessary to adapt plans to fit these individuals, to take a long-term view of them and ensure that they progress as fast as they are capable through the lower levels.

The problem is partly due to the need to transfer or amend duties for these staff as frequently as at six-monthly intervals, as they ride up over assignments. This may seem unreasonably short, but letting them remain in a post for a year or more leads to conflict and frustration. Yet, in spite of the problems created by these 'prima donnas', their contribution to a job over six months may often be very substantial. Ability to look at everything from first principles, to adapt, reshape and improve, often leaves a post in a far more effective shape.

Within reason, these people benefit from special assignments, investigating something and perhaps helping to get it back on the rails. Selected assignments to match broadening requirements are likely to be of value to both the company and the individual, and can often be created at short notice to fill a gap between operational assignments.

In conclusion, the policy of adapting plans to fit individuals takes on an extreme form when dealing with 'high fliers'. The organisation willing to devote the extra time and effort to these people is likely to find that it pays off handsomely.

Individual planning profiles

As part of the preliminaries for career planning, profiles of staff with potential abilities provide a useful aid during the planning discussions. These profiles give a fairly complete background history of the employee, covering his education, training and employment, his successes and failures, an assessment of his progress, and an appraisal of his possible future in broad terms. Figure 9.6 shows a profile of this type.

A valuable audit on overall career planning is provided by making extracts from the forward plans to show the detailed career development proposed for each individual. A career plan which appears on a sequence of entries on different charts may look far less logical when brought together on one sheet, and may reveal an inadequate period of development, or some other inconsistency which can be smoothed out.

Rate of development

Between career planning and salary planning there is a close link which I propose to use as a base for a series of thoughts which I think are very relevant to career planning.

Analysis of a large number of individual salary progression lines, especially if corrected for inflation, shows up an interesting pattern,

Stanley Neal JACKSON

Born: *12 August 1945 (33 in 1978)*
Married: *2 children*
Qualifications: *BSc Economics*

A short, stocky man, 5'7", 170 lb, generally well groomed, quietly dressed, glasses for reading, mild Devon accent.

High intellect, high verbal skills - articulate, highly numerate. Warm, mildly extrovert personality. Good at social graces. Well balanced - stable, no evidence of psychiatric trouble, high stress tolerance.

Education: *Plymouth Grammar School to 1964. London School of Economics to 1967 - pass degree in economics.*

Career: *Took a short-service commission in the RAF Education Branch and became a station education officer. Decided not to remain in the Service and sought an industrial education appointment in 1970.*

Joined xxxxxx company as an assistant training officer and was transferred to assistant personnel officer at the end of the year. He was moved around to a number of assignments in the personnel department during 1971 and appointed personnel officer for a small factory (400 employees) at the beginning of 1972.

He was engaged on all aspects of personnel work, but under heavy-handed central guidance, and left to become personnel manager of xxxxxx company, a small independent engineering firm, in June 1973.

His contribution to this post was substantial. He developed a rational approach to all personnel matters and 'sold' this by formal and informal training at all levels.

Promoted to Head Office shortly after we took over his unit in November 1974, he became group training manager. He virtually created our whole supervisor and management training activity and is playing a part in planning development of individuals.

Future: *Substantial potential evident. His work on specialised training courses has broadened him and an assignment on production planning from October next will be the first of three leading to appointment as manager of one of the smaller units in 2-3 years.*

Figure 9.6 Career profile for management development and succession

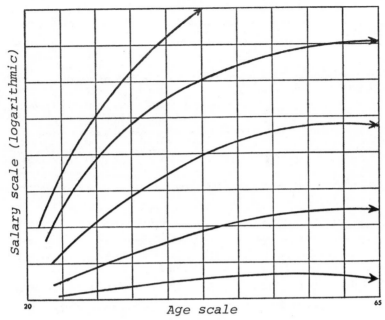

Figure 9.7 Percentile lines - graduates'
salary distribution

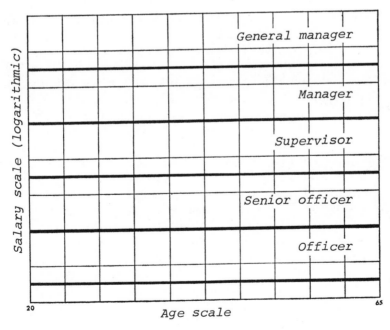

Figure 9.8 Salary levels for job levels

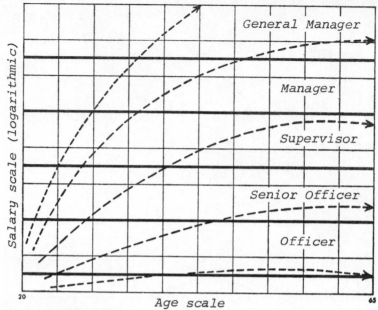

Figure 9.9 Career and salary progression rates

fanning up and out from comparatively closely related starting points. This picture can be seen from percentile distribution charts of particular categories, such as engineers' salaries in their periodic surveys, salary scatter charts covering young graduates, the Glacier Project findings, and so on. Figure 9.7 shows a distribution of a large number of graduates' salaries.

Salary levels tie in with the market values of jobs in a stratified form, as shown in Figure 9.8, higher salary being associated with increased job responsibilities in a higher position.

Superimpose Figure 9.7 over 9.8, as we have done in Figure 9.9, and we get an interesting picture. Putting aside salary planning until the next chapter, we have associated career and salary progress patterns for employees of differing capacity growth rates. The individual capable of achieving general manager level must break out of the lower levels as quickly as possible, rising from level to level as quickly as he gets on top of his responsibilities at the lower one. The individual rising only to the position of manager is slower off the mark and slower to make the step up from level to level.

Accepting that these lines are heavily smoothed out from a collection of irregular individual progress rates, it would seem that there is some relationship between rate of movement in the initial career years and subsequent potential. I would oppose the use of this as an operational rule, as the incidence of changing career growth is very high. An individual may develop late, or become motivated differently; he may work extremely hard until he exhausts his capacity and tails off; his efforts may vary from year to year.